PRAISE BY SOFIE'S

"Sofie provided a Creativity Workshop ᵢₒᵣ 4ᵤ staff from our psychological therapy service, which was full of experiential learning and was presented with warmth, curiosity and optimism. The content was based on sound psychological principles. We were shown how sometimes thinking patterns default and response styles can limit, rather than facilitate, creative thinking. As well as increasing our insight into the content and consequences of our thinking styles, we all stepped (not too far!) out of our comfort zones and had fun together as a team."

Dr Dale Huey AFBPsS, Consultant Clinical Psychologist, NHS

"Sofie's workshop was very effective in reinforcing the importance of creativity in business and clearly illustrated how vital creative thinking and innovation really is in producing results for long-term business success. Sofie is a superb communicator and motivator. She is an inspiring business leader who is a committed and passionate individual who genuinely cares about the success of what she is involved in and the people she is working with. She always goes the extra mile and gets people enthused and engaged in what she is doing."

Rene Mance, Computer Software Professional

"I found the workshop inspiring and it challenged some preconceptions I had about creativity and innovation. It also showed me how some companies are not after change, and this truly reflects in their behaviour and the way they don't invest in creative thinking ("yes but" people). It made me really think about the creative process and how to nurture new ideas. Companies looking for effective ways to encourage creativity in their staff should most definitely seek out Sofie and book one of her workshops."

Jessica Mo, Creative manager, Daydream studios

"Sofie is an inspiration to work with. I learnt so much by working with her, not least in terms of digital marketing — but also about the benefits of a positive attitude, believing in your product and working your socks off to share the good news about it!"

Grainne McGuinness, TV Producer/Director, Indee Productions

"Sofie has a wealth of knowledge in social media and digital marketing. She is patient, caring, reliable and very good at explaining how things can be done. She is supportive and always inspires me to do my best and make progress. She is an excellent coach."

Mahin Driskill, Author

"Sofie is a charismatic, insightful and smart digital marketer. I brought her in to my team to test and set up new marketing techniques, which she took up with gusto. She is eager to learn and research the subject and shares findings with colleagues enthusiastically. She inspires people around her with her work ethos and her get up and go. She's a pleasure to work with."

Santa Marku, Head of Marketing, BSI Business Information

Sofie and I met via a mutual colleague. Her knowledge and expertise in digital media was evident from my first meeting with Sofie. We went on to deliver a joint event for Women Entrepreneurs titled: Boost Your Online Profile. Since then Sofie has given me an insight into social media, but more importantly the confident message to try and try again until I find my online voice. I would recommend Sofie to anyone looking for a personal digital media /social media coach.

Gurnam Selvarajah, Co-founder, Women Entrepreneurs

BONUS RESOURCES

I am sure you will enjoy reading this book.
On a regular basis I will update the bonus page
with extra business building and brand
development content.

To check out the resource page go to:
www.sofiesandell.com/bonus

I hope you enjoy
the book!
Sofie X

SOFIE SANDELL

DIGITAL
LEADERSHIP

HOW CREATIVITY IN BUSINESS
CAN PROPEL YOUR BRAND
& BOOST YOUR RESULTS

FastPrint
Publishing

www.fast-print.net/store.php

Digital Leadership: How Creativity in Business Can
Propel Your Brand and Boost Your Results
Copyright © Sofie Sandell 2013

ISBN 978-178035-694-5

Email: publisher@sofiesandell.com

This publication is designed to provide accurate and authoritative
information in regard to the subject matter covered. It is sold with
the understanding that the publisher is not engaged in rendering
legal, accounting, or other professional service.
If legal advice or other expert assistance is required, the services
of a competent professional should be sought.

Cover Design & Layout by David Springer.
Portrait photography by Asya Barskaya.
Paintings on the cover by Sofie Sandell.

Contents

ACKNOWLEDGEMENTS

Thanks to everyone who has helped with this project.

Len Allen for publishing help. Wendy Millgate for being my editor. David Springer for cover design. Asya Barskaya for portrait photography. Cherry for designing the images. My parents, Marita and Sören, thank you. Everyone who has encouraged me in the process, thank you!

I would like to thank everyone who has given feedback: Solveig Malvik, Sarah Beckwith, Alexandra Illsley, Lesley Young, Minter Dial, PA Ståhlberg, Vince Stevenson, David Bridle and Joe Howard. If I have forgotten anyone who assisted on this project, please note that it wasn't deliberate; a big thank you to you also.

Thank you to every single person I met and got to know when I was teaching and training people in digital strategies and creativity.

Also, a big thank you to all digital platforms where this book is available.

WHO SHOULD READ THIS BOOK?

This book is for people who are interested in learning more about the digital world, creativity and leadership, and how to use all three to move ideas forward to create a better world where ideas can grow and develop.

More and more digital opportunities are presenting themselves, and a leader intent on broadening their horizons should take advantage of all forms of digital media in combination with their creative talents.

We have many great opportunities to connect with each other around the globe and create prosperity and new solutions to problems around us. If you are not digitally oriented yet, I urge you to dare to be creative and find a way to learn more about the digital world, creativity and leadership. You never know if this could be the start of a new career and your next stream of income. Stay curious and keep on learning.

INTRODUCTION

A while ago I tweeted this: 'Social media is about people; embracing the way people connect. It's about sharing, helping and doing well!'

Do you agree with this statement?

Most of us have turned into global networkers by using social media and are connected to just about everyone on the planet. Whether you realise it or not, employers, colleagues and acquaintances we have just met are checking us out on Google. We all have an online profile. We are all connected through digital media. With digital media I mean information that can be transmitted in digitised format using the internet. It can be websites, podcasts, online videos, social media and so on.

This book is about why it makes sense to use our creative mindset and social media to enhance relationships, expand business borders and drive leadership. It will show you how you can bring creativity into your business when you explore digital opportunities.

By using the Digital Leadership and Creativity Leadership Principles that I present in this book, you will be more aware of how creativity works and what you can do to make the most of the resources you have around you. You can start a blog and communicate with every other internet user in the world with just a few clicks. You can make your voice heard by using new platforms and communication tools, or you can improve how you use the digital tools you already have.

I've been involved with digital media and marketing for over ten years, and now I teach and train people in these subjects. If you want to learn, have fun and be more productive then the digital world is for you.

In 2007 I had a conversation with someone I admire as a leader. He said: 'All successful organisations must use the latest digital techniques. You'll learn new ways about how to make a bigger impact by doing that.' This short conversation made a huge impression on me and I started exploring new digital opportunities more and more.

You can use digital platforms to connect with people all over the globe. Your idea might be just what your market has been waiting years for.

Leaders are responsible for wealth creation wherever they are active. By this I don't simply mean that they accumulate a lot of money in the bank; they also make sure their employees, customers and the organisations around them are benefiting from the work they do. By using the digital tools available, you can share your thoughts and ideas and inspire others to take action. Most digital tools can be used by anyone. They are democratic and available to both you and me.

I believe that organisations that aren't embracing digital media are missing out on the things they really want: the ability to make an impact, to create new opportunities, to achieve wealth, gain prestige and, most importantly, have the chance to become leaders who inspire others.

If you choose to stay outside digital media, you'll miss out on a lot of information. If you are in business and are not present in social media, your customers will think that you aren't interested in communicating with them. Missing out on this communication can have a detrimental effect.

It takes courage to use digital media well. By reading this book my hope is that you will dare to be creative and make the most of the digital world.

When we look around the corner at what's coming in the future, digital media should be on everybody's radar. If you're not there now, it's time for you to consider where to start. If you are using digital tools, it's time to step up and take control of them so that they are working harder for you.

Dare to be creative and use the digital tools that are there for you.

All the best and enjoy the book.

Sofie Sandell
London, UK

PART ONE

OUR DIGITAL WORLD

*"The chief enemy of creativity
is good sense."*

Pablo Picasso

01 THE DIGITAL WORLD AT A GLANCE

What do we mean when we talk about the 'digital world'?

The digital world includes all websites, email and social media such as Facebook, Twitter and LinkedIn. Banking and other daily services have gone digital. TV is digital in most countries and all our mobile devices (tablets, notebooks and smartphones, for example) are digital. When we sign a petition online, we do it digitally instead of putting our name on paper.

We can vote online instead of going to a specific venue. Companies email us surveys to ask for our opinion. As a customer you can give online feedback if you are happy or unhappy about something.

We are using new technical platforms and solutions to help us in our lives. Our homes are becoming digital and we are receiving more and more information through digital channels. The digital world is helping us to communicate, exchange information and give our opinions. It encompasses a lot and is essentially here to make our lives easier.

KIDS GO DIGITAL

Our future will demand technical savvy and our children will use digital devices every day for the rest of their lives. Scary!

A friend of mine has a son who is four years old. He is very aware that his family doesn't have an iPad and he nags his parents on a daily basis to buy him one. Another friend's 18-month-old daughter knows how to find the photos on my iPhone. All the children that I've met in the past couple of years know how to play games on their parents' Smartphones and iPads. Children are growing up with digital tools around them constantly and these tools are here to stay.

THE NEW ERA

Digital media is also about sharing knowledge and facilitating access to knowledge. Everybody who has a computer or other similar device can get access to global knowledge. Experts in all kind of areas now freely give away their insights and discoveries to anyone who is interested. You can learn and develop your knowledge of almost any subject by searching for it online.

It is very easy to share opinions with others using digital and social media. It is possible to build a community of like-minded individuals that are active worldwide with the digital tools now available.

Things we did offline 20 years ago we now do online, and this is thanks to electronic communication. We find new friends, peers and supporters online. Many people that I first connected with online I now meet with face-to-face on a regular basis. The friendships that started digitally are just as much based on trust and honesty as any of my offline relationships, maybe even more so as trust is more easily lost in the digital world than outside of it.

THE SOCIAL MEDIA FORCE

Social media in its early days consisted of email, intranet, wikis and internal chat systems. You exchanged information with others, shared your thoughts and concerns, and you let others contribute to the discussion.

Today, social media has developed exponentially and there are endless opportunities to use it. We share our daily life with our friends and strangers over a variety of networks. We use new technologies to create groups and forums. Companies use social media to recruit new staff members and attract new clients/customers. We share our opinions on social networks and want our peers to join us. We also use it as a learning tool. Every day millions of new connections are made online and it helps us to deepen the relationships we already have.

The thing is social media is not a one-way broadcasting system. It's a social two-way highway — the people around you can contact you and have a conversation with you, and vice versa. It is crucial for all organisations who want to build an online presence and want to be found online to utilise social media. It is the vehicle to engage with their connections and be at the front of their target audience's minds.

02 WHY SOCIAL NETWORKING ONLINE MATTERS

Social media and online networking works really well because, as human beings, we are naturally social. We want to interact with others, show our empathy for others and share the latest news. Every day we find out about news, events and birthdays with the help of the internet.

Today, in 2013, Facebook has over 1 billion accounts and Twitter has more than 500 million accounts. Every second, all over the world, people are interacting with each other and new people are joining new networks.

Sofie says: *"Online, long-distance friendships can often be as valuable as real life friendships. The power of words and encouragement is extraordinary!"*

HUMANS ARE SOCIAL

Interacting with others is a basic need for human beings. Our ability to network with one another, connecting with others outside our tribe, is one of the reasons why we have thrived as a species. That is why we are here today, why we have been able to progress through different phases of development.

Sofie says: *"Women are naturally better at communication, building relationships and connecting with people. Look at the top ten Twitter accounts; eight out of the ten are women. If you're a man, open up your feminine side and become a better networker who can harness your connections more effectively."*

If you look back in time to when we were hunters, we lived in caves. We lived in small groups and had to go out and hunt for food. Back then we could not supply food for more people than those in the tribe.

Then we came up with the idea of farming. We learnt how to harvest and how to put seed into the ground to grow. This gave us more food for more people and we could start to live in larger groups.

Our next big developmental step was industrialisation. This started in England about 200 years ago and then spread throughout the world. We were able to create machines powered by steam and tools made of refined metals. The average income increased and the population started to grow. More people moved into towns and cities for work. The transport systems improved through the creation of better roads, trains and canals. It was easier to transport food and the cost of food was lower.

Today we are living in a new era known as the 'knowledge era'. In parts of the world there is plenty of food and you can learn and share new recipes with one click online. You can order your food online and get it delivered directly to your house. What part does social media play when new products and services are developed? What will historians say about the social media revolution? I believe that we also will refer to this current era as the social and mobile era. I wonder what the next step will be in how we obtain food. Maybe a 3D printer will print our food for us?

SOCIAL MEDIA ENABLES EMPATHY

It is deeply programmed into our DNA to show each other empathy — it's what makes us human. This is made easier with the help of social networks and digital media where we can 'like', comment and share information with each other. If the train station is closed, it will be mentioned on Twitter immediately. If you have something to celebrate, you can share it with all of your friends almost instantly.

We want to know what's going on and most of us want to engage with others and let other people know what we're up to and even how we're feeling. I once felt down and posted on Facebook: 'I'm in big need of a virtual hug...' That evening I received over 50 hugs and several messages, and, yes, it made me feel much better.

Sofie says: *"Praise your network in public. Most people love public compliments. Say thank you on a friend's Facebook wall or tweet someone who has done something you admire. Make it visible and show others that you are a fan of theirs and that you care about them."*

We have tools such as mobile phones and computers that make it very easy for us to expand our network and interact with more people. I think this is one of the reasons we can become so dependent on social media and online information. We can't help it; we're programmed to connect with others and we want to stay connected to the people we like.

SOCIAL PORTRAITS

You have access to several online social networks where you can show who you are and what your interests are by building an online profile. Your online profile is a blueprint of who you are and what you stand for.

I have read many people's descriptions of themselves on LinkedIn, Facebook and on their own websites. Some people represent themselves accurately and you get a true and honest picture of who they are by reading about them. Some online profiles that I've come across, however, are not a true and honest match with the person. One particular individual that I first connected with online told the world how fantastic he was at networking and how great he was at connecting people and helping them to become better networkers. When I met him in real life, he was a very shy person who had no charisma at all. He was not being honest about who he was. Don't make the same mistake he did.

If you want to make an impact online, you must be truthful about who you are and what you believe in. Your online personality should reflect the real you. Authenticity and integrity are integral to your dealings with others and thus success in your business and personal life.

DIGITAL LEADERSHIP IN PRACTICE
- THE POWER OF MANY DIGITAL VOICES

Currently in the UK (March 2013), there is a large campaign for equal marriage rights for homosexual couples, and two of the bigger lobbying organisations are Coalition for Equal Marriage (www.c4em.org.uk) and Out 4 Marriage (www.out4marriage.org). These organisations are working in a very smart and digital way. I signed the Coalition for Equal Marriage petition a while ago. First, I went onto their website and I signed the petition. Second, I was given the opportunity to send an email to my local Member of Parliament, which I did with a few clicks.

After I signed the petition, I did not expect to receive a reply from anyone. Two weeks later I was very surprised when I received a written and signed letter from my local MP in which she thanked me for showing an interest and said that they were working on the issue and will vote on equal marriage rights in 2013.

The third step on the Coalition for Equal Marriage petition website directs you to Out 4 Marriage's website where you are asked to send in a short video about why you support equal marriage rights.

The video campaign on YouTube is made up of videos in which people express their opinions on equal marriage rights. This is a smart and very simple idea. Anyone with a Smartphone or video camera can record a message and share their opinion with the world. It's about participation and engagement. If the message is worth sharing, the campaign will get publicity. People love it when someone such as Boris Johnson, the Mayor of London, expresses an opinion on equal marriage rights. When he sent in his video, it was in the press the next day. This is a clever and innovative way to show how an online digital campaign influences traditional media and gives it new content to write about. This is also a great example of how you can use social media to influence the government. Going online and using all the digital opportunities available is a powerful way of having an interactive dialogue with many different stakeholders: the gay community, organisations, individuals and celebrities all over the world.

Twenty years ago we would have signed paper petitions. The campaigners would have lobbied to be seen on TV and to appear in national newspapers. Now, with digital tools, we can start the campaign online and you as a citizen can help out and influence your local politicians, all with a few clicks of a mouse. The campaigners behind the Out 4 Marriage campaign have shown a deep understanding of social media as well as strong leadership and creativity.

If you have a cause you believe in and want to stand up for, start learning about how to use digital tools, develop your leadership skills and make an impact. You can help and inspire thousands of people and give them hope that change is possible.

03 OUR WORLD NEED LEADERS!

Whose responsibility is it to lead, to create change, to create wealth?

There are thousands of books out there about leadership and I've been reading and studying the subject to try and dig into its secrets for a long time. I've also been a leader in numerous situations and have learnt from these experiences. I know what works, when people are engaged, and what prejudices we have concerning leadership.

My view is that leadership is for everyone. It is for businesses, politics, sports clubs, universities, schools and communities. It is for you. Everyone can make a difference and take on leadership responsibilities. We have leaders everywhere; leadership has nothing to do with titles. More and more people need to claim their power as leaders and influence others despite having no formal authority.

We need leaders to create wealth. Our world needs strong leadership to help people to understand that the world around us can change, that there is hope. I believe that one of the reasons we exist is so that we can work together to create something better.

Leadership can take many forms: from fighting for democracy in a country that doesn't have it, to starting a new IT project that will improve the workflow in a company. We need leaders to create wealth — for everyone. We see leadership in every corner of society.

We have more opportunities than ever to create change and express our opinions. With digital media you can take action today and make an impact in the world around you. In this book I'll teach you a few tips about how to do this and I will also encourage you to dare to be creative. Using your creative mind while exploring the digital world will help you reach the next level. You can explore digital opportunities alone and you can also do it as a team.

We have entered the knowledge era and have new digital tools to use to share our message. What does leadership have to do with it? It means that you as a leader can influence even more people and make a bigger impact by sharing your message online. Many of the rules that apply in the real world also apply in the online world. So, if it makes sense to do something offline, it is also likely to work online.

WHAT DO GOOD LEADERS DO?

What good leaders have in common is that they understand that they have to keep improving themselves. Life is a continuous process of development, and you're included in that. The world moves on and you have to follow suit. Even more than that, once you accept how the world is moving in this new era, you can lead the way in your sector. Being a leader means to lead the way.

What do leaders do?

Leaders:

- give us hope: they make us believe that we can create something better
- show us the way forward and what's around the corner
- get people engaged
- break the old patterns of doing things
- inspire us
- have credibility
- show guts
- see new possibilities
- make us trust them

We just love to love leaders.

Often the person who is the leader is seen as the odd one out, the outsider doing something different. However, within a few years everybody is doing the same thing. I love the leadership lessons Clive Woodward shares in his book Winning. He was the first coach to get the national rugby players for England to work on their fitness with an aerobics instructor and he introduced the concept of changing to a new, clean shirt at half-time. It doesn't sound like a breakthrough today, but he started the trend and now it is common practise.

Leadership in big organisations

It will be stormy around you when you are changing something:

- You will be surrounded by smart people who know how to look after themselves.
- There will be a variety of conflicts that you will have to handle.
- The people around you will challenge you.
- You will face complex tasks every day.

It sounds great to be a leader, doesn't it? I have a lot of respect for those who manage to be a leader and help us shape the future.

HOW TO CREATE LEADERS

This is a crucial question for everyone. If society isn't creating good leaders for the future, where will we end up? If you look at how leadership/management development works in most companies today, you will find that people move to a managerial position in order to get a pay raise. Many of the people getting promotions are not interested in or equipped to lead others. They are promoted without much training in how to lead others and do not understand what is expected from them.

Most companies have middle managers in these positions because of the lack of structure in moving people up the career ladder. Is this really creative in the 21st century? I have friends who, without any management training and very little motivation, have been asked to lead and manage a team. Putting unmotivated people in charge of managing others is obviously a bad idea, but this is exactly what happens in a lot of companies.

A graphic designer friend was promoted to lead a big website project because he had the technical skills. He was doing alright but he lost part of his creativity due to the strain of leading the project. It was just not in his interests or in his personality to take on the job. He was not motivated to do the hours of administration that were included in the role. He learnt new skills and he can now move on to other big projects, but the cost was that he lost a big part of his own creativity.

Sofie says: *"Great leaders tell the world WHY they are doing what they are doing; not just what they are doing and how they are doing it."*

ARE LEADERS BORN OR ARE LEADERS CREATED?

I've read and heard this question far too many times. I have met leaders in all of the organisations that I've worked and been active in. Some of them came across as natural leaders and some grew into their roles. You can never say that you are born to lead; that just doesn't sound sensible to me. You don't know whether you are a good leader for a certain organisation or group until you have tried it for a decent length of time. Leadership goes in cycles. Don't judge the result until you have experienced all the seasons. Nonetheless, that's what people do.

When I was the president of Junior Chamber International (JCI) London in 2008, I undertook practical leadership training that lasted for a year. I gained new insights every week. One thing that I learnt about myself and others is that you have to make the most of your character and personality. Nobody will follow you if you do not do your job with integrity and honesty. We have to be true to ourselves. This is universal.

Sofie says: *"Leaders aren't afraid of being themselves online. They share their thoughts and ideas and are honest about what they believe in. This is the kind of person we find attractive and want to connect with."*

Develop your own style and learn how to connect with the people around you. How you do this is up to you, but you have to connect. As president of JCI London, I was very active in social media and I sent out a weekly newsletter. It took true commitment to do this and I changed the perception that many people had of the organisation. Many people thought JCI London was a dull and corporate organisation rather than a great network for young professionals. I was sending out this message online every week and we became more attractive to the public and more people joined us. We gained more members because we communicated with them online and tripled the number of visitors to our website. I was proud of my achievements when I handed the leadership over at the end of the year.

I once had a manager who didn't even say good morning to our team. How can you connect with them then? Didn't he know that it's good manners to say good morning? The message he was sending was that he was too important to say hello. His leadership style was not very efficient and he had huge problems engaging the team. The same rule applies online. If you never say hello to your network, it's hard to engage it. You need to show that you believe in and enjoy being a digital leader.

By the way, having a really bad boss will make you appreciate your good bosses even more. So say thank you to the arseholes you've met along the way. They've helped you to see the full scale of what is good and bad.

Sofie says: *"Being able to connect with others and build rapport is key if you want to make an impact and build sustainable relationships."*

DIGITAL LEADERSHIP IN PRACTICE - STARBUCKS

Some organisations show the way forward for others, and one example is the coffee chain Starbucks.

Early on they decided to be a business leader online and invested a significant amount of money and resources into being a digital-friendly coffee shop. I wonder how many people go to Starbucks every day in order to work and use their facilities as though it were an office. There are thousands for sure.

Starbucks is a social brand online and they have over 30 million fans on Facebook and over 3 million followers on Twitter (March 2013). When you buy something in Starbucks, you can pay with your mobile phone, which speeds up the payment process.

They keep their customers coming back through the use of a loyalty programme, and you can top up your Starbucks card with cash and then use it in the shops. They have an app for Smartphones and they are very keen to try out new digital opportunities.

I choose to go to Starbucks to work on my computer because I know that they will have an electrical socket available. When I go to other coffee shops there are often not enough, if any, sockets available. Starbucks has got the basics right. In the beginning of the sit-in-coffee-shops-and-work era, Starbucks was not afraid of letting people sit down and work for hours. Other coffee shops were suspicious of guests with computers, and some of them even had rules about how much you had to spend to sit there.

I live near a Starbucks and every time I go there the staff are happy and friendly. As a customer it is an awesome experience to visit their café. When I am in the area, I am likely to go to Starbucks just because the staff are great.

Starbucks has over 18,000 stores in over 50 countries and they use digital techniques to help them with their expansion. They appointed a Chief Digital Officer in 2012, and this is a trend that we will see more companies adopt in the future. Companies, their boards and executives all need to take the digital challenge seriously and that means that a senior leader should be employed to look strategically at all digital development.

The sockets in Starbucks make them a more digital-friendly coffee shop compared with their competitors. They've got the basics right. (Photo published with permission from Starbucks)

04 YOUR DIGITAL WORLD IS CREATIVE!

For me creativity is a way to relate to problems and challenges in work and life. When you take the creative route you don't take the most obvious path from A to B. You choose a path that will involve something that is unfamiliar or new to you. Creativity is about trying out new things, new combinations. It is the combining of objects, people and challenges that would normally not be brought together. One example is a customer relationship game that I conduct in my workshops. I ask the participants to come up with some challenges they are struggling with. In the next step we add a new object into the discussion; it can be any random thing. Then they have to try to solve the problem with the help of the random object.

An example is when a group of people tried to come up with a new approach to a global product for the construction industry. They used random nouns from a dictionary and had to use them when coming up with ideas. In this case they used the words 'soldier', 'handbag' and 'paper'. This made them come up with a new solution that had nothing to do with their former ideas. It is great fun to look for a solution this way, and your mind is pushed to think outside normal patterns.

The environment in which you are active plays a big part in your creativity and how you can express it. If you are in an environment that discourages creativity, there is a risk that you are going to feel stuck and less creative. When people I meet say that they are not creative, I think that some of them define creativity as something that is reserved for authors, artists, children and people in creative jobs. But creativity is something that we all use when we work together with others, in all situations in life and at work.

When we use the first and most obvious solutions that come to mind when we solve a problem, we are quickly getting it over and done with. It sounds good to do it this way, but we are not stretching or developing ourselves. It can of course work well in some cases to take the easiest route, but it's not inviting any new thinking; you are using your old pattern. If you are trying to change something, you should look into different paths and stay open to new solutions.

In school we're taught to solve problems as quickly as possible, and if we do this well, we're praised, people clap their hands and we're given a gold star. This solution is quick, but it's not exploring any new perspectives and it's not necessarily the best solution. This forms a pattern where we continue to look at problems in this way. There is not much conscious reflection for creativity and innovation.

When you're being creative, you're not taking the easiest and most obvious route when you're going from A to B. You're using a new focus, seeing new opportunities; it is as if you're looking at the problem from another planet.

Here are two examples of creativity that you can use in your everyday life. If you are always looking in the same kind of shops when you are buying new clothes, take a day when you are only allowed to visit shops you have never been shopping in before. Next time you are cooking, why not try something you have never dared to cook before. You may well discover a great shop and cook an amazing meal when doing this.

This is what creativity means to me — allowing yourself and your team to explore new ideas and solutions. It's often when you make a mistake that you're innovating and creating a new way of thinking. By making a mistake when you are cooking a dish you never tried before, you can discover a new amazing dish. Creativity is pushing you forward.

*"One of the great joys of life is creativity.
Information goes in, gets shuffled about, and
comes out in new and interesting ways."*
Peter McWilliams

A classic example of creativity and accidental learning is how Alexander Fleming discovered penicillin 1928. He returned to his lab after a vacation and was going through a pile of dishes. He noticed something strange about one of them. While he had been away, a mould had grown on it and it seemed that this particular mould had the killer bacteria Staphylococcus Aureus growing on it. At this time in 1928 Fleming was looking for a new drug to kill bacteria and his research and experience made him see that this had the potential to do that. His discovery was not an instant hit; it took until 1940 to develop the new drug. Two scientists at Oxford University were using new chemical techniques and methods and they found a way to produce the drug. Since then penicillin has saved millions of lives.

Sofie says: *"It can be your mistake or flaw that
makes us discover the solution for
big problems and issues in the world.
Don't be afraid of making mistakes;
they will help you to see the world
from a new perspective."*

ANYONE CAN BE CREATIVE — AND IT'S FREE!

Creativity is free and it is the solution to many of the problems that we struggle with every day. Every person can be creative, and if you don't believe that you were born to be creative, I can assure you that you can learn to be creative. It's within all of us.

Whenever I'm training people in creative thinking and creativity, there are at least a few people who say out loud that they are not creative and have never been a 'creative'. They are labelling themselves by verbalising it, and when doing this often they start believing it. I share my view of creativity and we discuss why they think that they are not creative. At the end of the training, they leave believing that they have the creative power inside them. They just have to look a bit deeper within themselves and stop saying that they are not creative. We are all creative and we can learn how to be even more creative.

Look around you and all the structural problems there are in many of the ecosystems we are living in: transport, pollution, education, healthcare and banking. These huge ecosystems are in need of transformation and politicians discussing how to solve these problems doesn't seem to be the most efficient solution.

I truly believe that a good dose of creative thinking can bring the changes needed for these systems. Politicians and leaders are approaching problems by just going round and round in the same circle — not much new will come out from the discussions and meetings. Most of them probably don't have access to the creativity tools that can help them progress.

CREATIVITY AS A NATURAL BOOSTER

Being creative is to see what is possible in situations when others see only problems. People's natural abilities are strengthened as they seek solutions, which is good for productivity, teamwork and profits.

Combining a deep understanding of your market and your customers with creative thinking can transform your business and product offers. Stay passionate about the creative process and learn how it works and you'll be more successful.

CREATIVITY DECISIONS

Make a decision and create your own destiny. 'Should I or should I not' will never make your creative mind flourish. I've often been in situations where I don't know what to choose. I've spent hours and days thinking about choices and felt stuck.

A specific situation I remember is when I set up my business; what shall I do? I had many interesting opportunities I could focus on, but I knew that without focus you can't sell your services. It took me almost two months of contemplation before I made my choice. When I made it, my structure and website was set up in a few days and a few weeks later I had my first three clients. Action will create your destiny.

CREATIVITY MAKES YOU ATTRACTIVE

We love to work with positive and creative people. A creative person is like the honey pot that all bees are drawn to. Do your best and attract other great people who want to work with you. You might end up changing the world together.

I have heard that you'll look younger for longer if you are using your creativity more often. It must be connected with having fun while you are being creative and working around positive people. You can say that creativity is a great and cheap anti-wrinkle cream.

DIGITAL LEADERSHIP PRINCIPLES

- Social media is here to stay. Learn how to use the tools.

- We love to interact with each other and social media makes it easier.

- With a few words online you can share your thoughts and help others.

- Be a good friend online and follow the social rules that apply in real life. They apply in both the online and offline worlds.

- Develop your leadership skill on a continual basis.

- Creativity is a very cost-effective resource and it's free for anyone to use.

PART TWO

DIGITAL LEADERSHIP

"Creativity requires the courage to let go of certainties."

Erich Fromm

05 THE LANGUAGE OF CREATIVITY

The language and words you use are powerful. They help you set directions and goals for yourself and the people you have around you. I would like to share some of my thoughts about how to foster creativity in your team and organisation. All organisations need to be innovative today and creativity is relatively cheap to invest in compared to recruiting new staff, IT, buildings and other assets.

If you do the same thing in business year after year, that may not satisfy your customers. When growing you need to be creative in developing new solutions that keep clients coming back for more. Creativity is a real business advantage and your clients notice this when working with you.

In most people's day jobs, creativity is about how you create something together as a team when working on a product or project. There are many critical aspects in managing teams and in this example I will focus on a digital team. When working I've observed that many teams are stuck in non-productive patterns. The result is that objectives are not met due to poor communication and lack of knowledge about sharing and supporting new ideas. Staff members are hesitant to be creative, and it is not the individuals' fault; it is a flaw in the culture and a lack of awareness of how creativity, ideas and innovation work.

If your organisation is looking into how it can grow and reach a new market, it is likely that the ideas that come up will involve digital media. It is with new technology that you can reach more people. If you are not aware about how to handle new ideas, you might kill new ideas by mistake.

STAKEHOLDERS TEND TO HAVE DIFFERENT INTERESTS AND AGENDAS

Looking at digital efforts from the human resources perspective, you have the content creators, web editors, e-commerce managers, sales people, business analysts, technical experts, developers, designers, image editors ... you name it!

There are numerous key functions to keep a great digital environment alive. Each team is also likely to have its own agenda about what is required and how it should be accomplished. Many digital teams I know find it challenging to achieve effective collaboration.

I was once working on a company's global website and Google's ability to find the website was compromised due to duplicated content on the company's local websites. This made it hard for Google to show an accurate result and the content, which was similar, was competing against each other. To change this took a lot of effort and people from several countries had to agree about how to move forward. Part of the solution was to design a better landing page, on which a user could choose the site for their country or region.

People have different ways of looking at problems and diverse views about what the priorities and solutions are. This often creates conflicts and these disagreements can drain the energy in the organisation.

DARE TO SAY YES TO IDEAS

To avoid the problem of inter-departmental tension and many other problems, I would like to introduce you to the concept of saying 'yes' to ideas — to keep the creativity level high and the flow of ideas continuing. This approach is used in many successful organisations. Are you familiar with Pixar Studios? They use this method and all of their staff are trained in how to promote creative flow.

In essence, this concept means that when someone has an idea, you should say 'Yes, and...' Be open to the idea and let the person continue to tell you more about their idea.

Too often people are in the habit of saying 'Yes, but...' This 'Yes, but...' often continues with 'Yes, but we did this last year', 'Yes, but I'm not really sure if that will work', or 'Yes, but we're so busy so at the moment we're not able to do that.'

Do you see what I see? This 'Yes, but...' is a no in disguise.

All of these 'but' comments drain people's energy, make them less motivated to share and explore their ideas, and make it less likely that their ideas will become reality. Some of us would say that you are creating a negative energy.

When you say 'Yes', and you are open, you are encouraging what's coming next. You are happy to improvise with what's served. 'Yes, and, I would like to know more about your research...' This answer would get the person to tell you everything about it, share all stories and insights, and that is what you are after, right?

Take a day or an evening and look at yourself; how many times do you use the phrase 'Yes, but...' in a sentence. How many times do the people around you say the words 'Yes, but...?' If you are honest, you will conclude that it is a lot more often than you previously thought.

When an idea is in someone's head, it is just an idea. It is when you're exploring, implementing the concept and doing something about it, that you're truly innovating. To effectively execute an idea you need your colleagues' support. The best way to gain this support in the early stages of developing an idea is to be positive and utilise 'Yes and...' energy.

> I never made one of my discoveries through
> the process of rational thinking.
> **Albert Einstein**

FLOODING IN OPPORTUNITIES

Digital teams have endless opportunities to try new tools and techniques, but they are also likely to have limited resources. When individuals get into the mindset of saying 'Yes, but...' they are inclined to turn down ideas that should be acted upon. In the digital world, there is often that additional 10% of ideas that will provide the extra push to convert your visitors into raving fans, thereby driving sales growth. You will achieve higher conversion rates and drive more traffic to your site. Your site will become a portal of live and constantly evolving information, which customers are likely to visit on a regular basis.

I've worked with many different teams and a huge difference was made when the internal language was changed. When you say 'Yes and...' you get amazing results. Just changing this tiny word 'but' to 'and' makes a world of difference.

I've also worked in more negative teams. In those situations everything seemed to take forever, and the results were not impressive. Team members and leaders said 'Yes, but...' to each other all the time.

When I worked at BSI (British Standards Institution), in the business information publishing division in London, we had many external trainers coming in every year to give us training. It was focusing both on the technical and content aspect of e-commerce and marketing. One year I attended creativity training outside of work and suggested that our team should hire a creativity trainer and teach us more about the 'Yes, and...' principles. Two months later the creativity trainer was teaching us how creativity works. The result was amazing and we used a different language after that. The team members got tools to use and we could identify when our language and behaviour were working against us. We improved our workflow and used fewer resources, which was a result we were very pleased with.

Sofie says: *"When you change the language you use when speaking to your colleagues, you help the group energy to flow smoother, and new creative ideas will start coming to you."*

WHY IT IS WORTH IT

Every time you can do something that makes your website visitors' experience easier, clearer and more engaging, you'll earn more money. When an improvement is implemented, it's finished and people don't have to think about it any longer.

Taking action creates space for new ideas and improvements, and you and your colleagues are more likely to be in a productive flow.

Sofie says: *"Digital creative leaders let go of the old and make space for the new to expand."*

THE END RESULT

Improvements in the case of a website ultimately mean that your current and potential customers will have a better experience. An easy and painless user experience is crucial to the success of all websites and digital platforms. When a site is cumbersome and frustrating, your prospective customer will leave your site and go to a competitor. They will spend time and money there instead — which is a company's worst nightmare.

When you and your colleagues start saying 'Yes, and...' to new ideas and stop saying 'Yes, but...' you're creating positive energy. You're creating a culture that encourages and nurtures new ideas; people will feel empowered when someone is listening to them.

I encourage you to give it a try. Say 'Yes and...' and let the conversation flow. Your colleagues will love you!

CREATIVE LEADERSHIP PRINCIPLES

· Use: 'Yes, and...' instead of 'Yes, but...'

· Be nice to new ideas and be positive. Use a sign saying 'Handle with care' if the idea is new

· Keep telling your colleagues positive reinforcements about their ideas. The more you say yes, the more likely you are to push people in the right direction

· When being a 'nice guy' you'll be like a honey pot attracting all the bees. People will feel drawn to you and they will want to share their ideas. It is a real honour to be in this position, and you're creating a lot of power around you!

06 CREATIVITY IN BUSINESS
- IMPROVISE OR BECOME INSTITUTIONALISED

C reativity and the ability to handle ideas nicely matters in business and will continue to differentiate the successful businesses from those that are left behind. Aren't organisations around the world creative? Yes, some organisations are, but when an organisation stops being creative they risk becoming a stuffy place where everything takes forever to get done.

Organisations that are left behind have a mindset of 'Yes, but...' and are not willing to learn anything new. New fresh ideas are not seen as a valuable asset and the organisation is not listening to their employees or their customers. They have become what I call 'insti-tutionalised'.

The environment and culture you create for yourself and your team to work in will matter. When I'm teaching creativity, one big part is how you're handling new ideas, and how you and your team, organisation and the whole system work together. I've heard many times, 'We have tried that before and it didn't work.' What this really means is that the people who did it then couldn't make it work. It has nothing to do with you and your abilities. If anyone is negative to your idea or suggestion, it means that they can't see how it will work. What they say is not the whole truth.

Sofie says: *"Successful creative people have identified who their biggest supporters are and they ask them for help and feedback on a regular basis."*

A former colleague stopped developing a new marketing campaign just because his boss pulled a funny face when he presented it. Could he be sure that his boss's face really meant that it was a bad idea? Or could he just have had something else on his mind? I suggested that he should ignore the funny face and continue developing the idea, which he did. After a few weeks in the incubator, he launched his marketing campaign and everybody he needed help from bought into the concept and his boss loved it.

Do you think in the same pattern as the person in the example above? Do you dare to change your own thinking pattern? Are you just slightly improving what you have? To be great and stand out today you need to do things differently. Doing things differently means that you have to open up the creative resources you have both within you and your organisation.

"Creativity is the ability to see relationships
where none exist."
Thomas Disch

YOU'RE RESPONSIBLE FOR YOUR OWN CREATIVITY

You have your personal creativity, your team's creativity, organisational creativity and the creativity in the ecosystem where you belong. Creativity takes many shapes and forms and is present in all stages in your life.

You're personally responsible for feeding your creativity, and it's wise to review what helps you get into a better flow. Do the exercise Setting Your Conditions for Creativity in Chapter 21 to get to know what works best for you. We are all different and there is no solution that fits all.

Team creativity can be tricky. This is the type of creativity that you and your team are most likely to work with. Most of us are not artists and writers working by ourselves. We're part of a bigger system and we should learn how it works and how we can improve in it.

ASK YOURSELF:

- How do I handle new ideas in my team? Am I handling them in a nice way or am I killing many new ideas in their early stage?

- Can my organisation welcome creative thinking in a better way? Or am I stuck in old patterns?

- How is the system around me working? Do I need to tackle a structural problem with a creative solution?

- Is the system I'm working in holding me back and do I feel that it's impossible to innovate and bring new creative solutions to the table?

"I love how people in this business push themselves to know themselves, the world, and their creativity better."
Josh Lucas

The diagram on the previous page represents the creativity of the ecosystem in which you work. The first circle represents you. You have to learn about yourself and your personal creativity first; you are the focus of your own creativity. Then you have the team creativity — how well the team members are working creatively together. The third circle represents the organisation's awareness of how to make creativity flow better between the teams. The last circle is the ecosystem in which you are working. Is it the educational, retail, health care ecosystem you are active in? How open is the ecosystem to new ideas? How have the rules changed over the last 10 years in the ecosystem? Your team can be part of a very slow organisation, but you still have many opportunities to be creative and develop new ideas.

Sofie says: *"Creative leaders dare to improvise with the resources they have available. There's no need to bring in external consultants to deliver a long report about what should be done just because no one in the team dares to say it. They trust that the people in their team and organisation will find a solution to the problems they face."*

HOW TO HANDLE IDEAS NICELY

When you dare to say yes to new ideas and you're starting to use creativity principles, you're unleashing an enormous amount of power. Dare to improvise with what's on offer. How can you make the most out of the opportunities you have around you? I've said it before, but the 'Yes, and...' are some of the most powerful words in the universe.

There are many good strategies of work that you can use to get this flow working better. Here are some examples:

· Treat all ideas with respect from the start. Like the ugly duckling they might just transform into the most beautiful creature you can imagine.

· Give your colleagues/partners positive feedback every day.

· Have regular team meetings so people learn to share what they are doing and update each other on projects.

· Stay in a conscious state of mind as often you can.

*"The major problem is that creative
ideas are evaluated as soon as you have them.
That's completely wrong. A creative idea that you like, or
your business likes, must first be developed on its own
terms. Then, and only then, can you evaluate
it and see what it can do in the real world."*
PA Ståhlberg

THE ORGANISATIONAL LIFE-CYCLE

You can compare an organisation with the life of a human. When a start-up is born, they're curious and hungry, and when growing up they enter different stages in life.

BABY

The start-up is finding its way around, exploring and having fun. You don't know what to expect at this stage, and every week there is massive progress and learning taking place. The first years are fundamental and you're developing the organisational culture, and the culture you're creating will follow the organisation when it's growing.

TEENAGER

Then in the next stage the organisation becomes a teenager and is slightly more resistant to change. Still finding their own style and how things work, teenagers are cheeky and won't listen to 'experienced' adult advice. They do things the way they feel is right and they like to chill and relax. They also love hanging out with their peers online.

Examples of teenagers: Facebook, Amazon, Apple, Twitter, Expedia, Top Shop, Virgin Atlantic, Ryanair, Easy Jet, TED.com, eBay, Skype and PayPal.

ADULT LIFE

Later the organisation has turned into an adult and they know what they like and are less likely to change. If anyone wants to change something in the organisation, it will take time and change will be met with resistance. They are likely to adapt to the digital solutions that are available, but they are not sure how to make the most of them.

Examples of adults: Marks & Spencer, British Airways, General Electric, and Tesco.

BECOMING AN OLDIE

Some organisations reach the stage of being an oldie and they know what they like for breakfast, lunch and dinner. They are not likely to listen to new ideas and the whole organisation is at risk of being left behind, something that some employees are painfully aware of but they are not listened to. These organisations have not embraced any recent innovation or change and are struggling to explore new markets.

These companies are often mentioned as being oldies in my workshops: Nokia, HMV, BP, Philips, Blockbuster (video store in the UK that went bust January 2013)

WHAT DO TEENAGERS HAVE IN COMMON?

The most successful organisations in the world are in the teenage category. Often a participant in my workshops points out that they all are using technically advanced systems, which is true. The businesses in the teenage group always use advanced internet technology and love to be present in the digital world, but this is not the whole picture. I will explain a bit more about what else they have in common.

TECHNOLOGY AND THE INTERNET

Many companies in the world have access to internet and advanced technology, and everyone can explore creativity and the creative leadership style. Creativity and great leadership are free; it doesn't cost much to explore and start practising. A company that is exploring new digital opportunities needs to invest in technology and their people. They also need to challenge how their business is working and how they fit into the bigger picture. Who are they working with in the ecosystem? How will they earn money in the future? Where do they see new opportunities?

> *"Curiosity about life in all of its aspects, I think,*
> *is still the secret of great creative people."*
> **Leo Burnett**

I used to have a Nokia Smartphone a few years ago and their digital platform for apps called Ovi drove me crazy; it was so bad and didn't work at all. My next phone was an iPhone and the user experience between these two phones is remarkable. Nokia didn't invest in a good platform and the iOS and Google Android platforms were miles ahead of them. Nokia then moved on and now use a new platform solution, but I and millions of Nokia customers still remember our frustration from using their old platform. That's an impression that will stay with me and the other unsatisfied Nokia users for many years ahead. Whatever cool advertising campaigns Nokia do in the future, they won't persuade me to try a Nokia again.

> *"Innovation has nothing to do with how many R & D dollars you have. When Apple came up with the Mac, IBM was spending at least 100 times more on R & D. It's not about money. It's about the people you have, how you're led and how much you get it."*
> **Steve Jobs, as quoted in Fortune 1998-11-09**

CHANGING THE WAY YOU MAKE MONEY

The teenage companies are changing how business is done within their ecosystem. They're leading the way on a path that others will later follow. They are trying out a new style and new outfit and are using the latest technology.

One of the teenage brands that I'm a loyal customer of is Amazon. I've been buying books from them for years and now I can instantly download Kindle books from their store. I also buy other random things and gifts from their vast web-shop.

They have made thousands of people publishers by opening up the ability to publish a Kindle book. And they are opening up their platform for millions of businesses to sell their products online.

RELATIONSHIPS ONLINE AND PLATFORMS

Amazon is embracing the ability to build a business relationship with anyone. There is no discrimination or selective process. They embrace openness and invite us to publish our books as Kindles and also use their e-commerce platform to sell our products. An example of this is the fact that I'm now publishing my book as a Kindle eBook and that wasn't possible just a few years back.

Facebook has opened up their platform to be used by any business in the world. Anyone can set up a fan page or group and start interacting with their customers. Through an Application Programming Interface (API) developers can integrate their products into Facebook and obtain more interactions between their websites and Facebook. Some companies that are doing this through API are: The Guardian (a UK newspaper), Pinterest, Eventbrite, TripAdvisor and Goodreads.

MixCloud is a digital music, radio and podcast platform that invites you to add your audio content online and with a few clicks to share it online. The platform can be used by anyone and you don't pay to use the service. It is a great way to share your content and build up your listener base. As a user you can choose what and when you would like to listen to the content, there are no restrictions.

Examples of innovative business platforms are: iTunes, Facebook, Twitter, LinkedIn, Eventbrite, Google Maps, Udemy, Mixcloud, YouTube, Vimeo, Google+ and Salesforce.com. They are inviting you and other businesses to contribute to their success by opening up their platforms.

VISIBLE LEADERSHIP

Many teenage companies have inspiring and visible leaders, many of whom you're likely to know by name. They want to be seen and are often social online. They know that their visibility is going to help their brand expand.

Have a look on Twitter for @RichardBranson, @GuyKawasaki and @Jacqueline_Gold. They all use Twitter to connect with fans and people all over the world. If it works for a super entrepreneur, an entrepreneur/author and a CEO, it could very well work for you.

In all workshops I've delivered, not many people know who the CEOs are among the companies in the oldies category. They have leaders who you can seldom find any information about online. Many of these CEOs don't even have a LinkedIn profile, so from the outside it looks as if they don't see themselves as an important part of the bigger picture.

One more thing many teenage companies have in common is that they have made a profit during the recession. They have managed to grow when others have experienced a tough time. Could it be because they are aware of the creativity principles or is it because they are using digital opportunities? The answer is a mix of many factors, but creativity and taking advantage of digital opportunities helped them.

Sofie says: *"Digital leaders know that they have to be visible in social networks online. Both as the person they are and as an organisation. If you're not, you'll be seen as invisible. Being present in social media is not only about driving traffic and converting leads, but first of all showing your clients, staff and network that you exist and are there to help them."*

THE CLOUD

Companies who are in the teenage category make the most of the cloud by using an advanced IT infrastructure and investing in flexible cloud solutions. This helps them to invest their resources in other projects and also gives them more freedom and mobility. They have access to their digital content wherever they are and they just pay for the space they use.

RELATIONSHIP BUILDING AND PARTNERSHIP

People all around the world are building connections online with each other. Many successful companies are inviting their customers to contribute to their products and services. A general example is when they invite developers to build new applications using their platform and technology.

I'm not a programmer or developer myself, but just the thought of building something for iPhone App store or Google Android makes me excited. There are many restrictions and rules that are set up to manage this process, but if you're playing within these you can be hugely successful.

INVITATIONS ARE DEMOCRATIC AND THE DOOR IS ALWAYS OPEN

In the past you had to know the right person to be invited to a business partnership. Many of the successful teenage businesses are inviting anyone to use their platforms for their business. Anyone can publish a Kindle book on Amazon. People all over the world can share their videos on YouTube and you can create a Google+ community and use Google Hangout for meetings. In fact, every person who has created a podcast or a great music-mix can upload it to Mixcloud. There is no need for an invitation any longer. The door is always open.

"When the flowers bloom, the bees come uninvited."

INTERACTION, FUN AND PLAY

Teenage companies are likely to hang out on each other's platforms. They are active in social networks, and they use an application programming interface (API) to connect platforms with each other. It's in their basic behaviour to share and keep each other updated online. Most people in their organisations want to keep the door open for interaction, fun and play.

THE ABILITY TO LISTEN TO FEEDBACK

Successful teenage businesses are not only building successful relationships and partnerships; they are also listening to feedback from their customers and employees. Eric Smith, the chairman of Google says that Google built their whole business on feedback.

So listen to what everyone around you tells you. A lot of information for business improvement can be found there. I heard from Nikhil Shah, one of the co-founders of Mixcloud.com, that they collect feedback in many ways, but speaking to users and content producers gives them the most insights into what their customers struggle with or what is on their wish list. By doing this they show their customers that they care and they are always improving their product.

One of my favourite restaurants in London is Sophie's Steakhouse in Fulham. I was once annoyed with the light in their toilet. The light made you look like a ghost. In fact, my friend and I thought we looked like we were going to be ill, until we realised it was the light. There were many customers who experienced the same light.

As many businesses do, Sophie's Steakhouse has a Facebook page. The next morning I wrote a comment about the lighting issue on their Facebook wall, and it took them one week to reply back to me. I felt as if they didn't care about my opinion about the lights. If you have an open wall where your customers will write and comment, you have to reply back quickly. From my point of view you need to reply back within a couple of hours if it's a normal work day. If you're not planning to let people interact with you on Facebook, you can remove the comment field from your page and only allow yourself to post on the wall. Not so social, but you're not giving them reason to feel as I did.

If a client is complaining about your service or product online, it isn't a disaster. In the case when I complained on Sofie's Steakhouse Facebook wall, I did it because I care about them and wanted to let them know. I've been to hundreds of bad restaurant toilets, but I don't complain on their Facebook page. In this case I really cared and wanted a response from them. Unfortunately, they took too long to reply to me, so I felt as if they ignored me. However, fortunately, when I next returned to the restaurant, I noticed that they had changed the lighting in the toilet.

A customer who complains online is most likely a very engaged customer, and if you can reply back to them and have a conversation, you are likely to have them back again. And they in turn are likely to tell their peers that you got back to them.

For over five year Starbucks has collected feedback from their customers online though the website http://mystarbucksidea.force.com where anyone can suggest ideas for improvement. To collect your customers' opinions is nothing new. What I particularly like about Starbucks' approach is that you can see how the ideas are coming along and that it has a community feel to it. Starbucks would fit into the teenage category and they are a leader in their field.

Sofie says: *"Being social and staying social with your customers is a unique way to develop your products. Your colleagues and your customers combined knowledge could hold the secrets to your future success. Creative leaders are great listeners!"*

SAYING YES TO IDEAS

Companies in the teenage category are open to new ideas, new ways of building a customer base and making money. They are building a culture that allows ideas to grow stronger before they evaluate them.

ALWAYS IN A LEARNING MOOD

The teenage organisations never stop learning; they explore new technology, partnerships and possibilities all the time. They encourage curiosity and time to reflect on ideas and problems.

Sofie says: *"Creative leaders attract talented people. They are likely to get the best to work with them."*

THE MUSIC INDUSTRY–SOME OLDIES AND SOME TEENAGERS

The music industry has resisted the digital change for many years. Many music giants spent a lot of time and money fighting illegal downloading while young entrepreneurs were inventing new solutions. Those that didn't invent with their customers but stayed with the old model lost out.

HMV, one of the biggest physical music stores in the UK, recently went bust. People around the business were predicting this for years, but they never changed. They stayed with their old concept and didn't change their business model. When they informed over 60 people that they were being made redundant, their social media manager Poppy Rose Cleere tweeted live from the @HMVtweets account telling the whole world what was going on in the room.

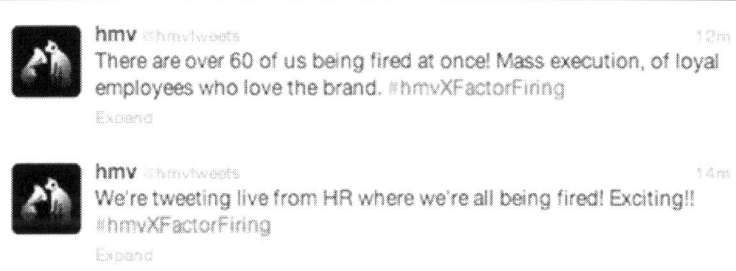

Their marketing director who was lucky to be staying in the company panicked and had problems accessing Twitter to remove what she said. The tweets that Poppy Rose Cleere wrote are still publicly available as screenshots, and that is a digital shadow that HMV will have to live with forever. Poppy Rose says on her private Twitter account that one reason she did this was to help the HMV executive to wake up and realise that social media matters. If they had been more willing to learn about social media and change their business model earlier, they might have survived.

> *"Innovation is the creation of the new or the re-arranging of the old in a new way."*
> **Michael Vance**

The newcomers in the music industry have invented new ways of listening to music. Spotify.com is a great way to listen to music. It's fun to click around finding new music and old songs you've not heard for years. You can download and listen to some music for free and you can subscribe to their services. I also love YouTube. Some days I use YouTube as my music player and it's hilarious when you find an old music video you have not watched for 20 years.

In December 2012, Gangnam Style, the viral hit from Korean pop-star PSY, became the first music video to reach more than 1 billion views on YouTube. Up until the end of 2012 Billboard, the music top list in the US didn't factor YouTube views in its ranking methodology. They were relying only on radio plays and paid purchases. But now, after Gangnam Style became a viral hit, they are including the number of times the songs have been played on YouTube.

We have so many new ways to listen to music today, digital radio stations, your Smartphone or iPod. As a Swede living in London, I miss Swedish radio and TV. Within two clicks on my iPhone I've access to Swedish radio and Swedish TV programmes. None of these solutions make money in the way music, radio and TV used to, and the solutions we use now were not around just a few years ago.

The companies who resisted the digital change, and didn't see that music was going digital, were digging their own grave. They didn't listen or watch what was going on in the world around them and then surprisingly their customers were spending their money elsewhere. To sum it up: they were not coachable or open to learning about new digital ideas. This led to a true massacre in the music industry.

PIXAR STUDIOS–A TEENAGE COMPANY

I'm a big fan of the Pixar movies Finding Nemo and Toy Story — I love them both. Pixar studios are known for being one of the most creative companies in the world and you can learn a lot from their film development process.

They have never bought a script from outside the company. All movie ideas were born and developed internally. They use the creative leadership principles that I'm writing about in this book, and you can use them too. They are applicable everywhere, whether it be developing a product, a service or a film.

> *"Every single Pixar film, at one time or another,*
> *has been the worst movie ever put on film. But we know.*
> *We trust our process. We don't get scared and say,*
> *'Oh, no, this film isn't working."*
> **John Lasseter, Chief Creative Officer at Pixar Studios**

Pixar says you don't know where you're going with a film — they describe it as opening a chest with a secret treasure. And all creative people who are involved contribute to making the film better. Every time someone has an idea how to improve the story or the process, their colleagues have to listen. They have to show each other respect and be open to new ideas.

Creativity at Pixar is about solving problems along the way. It is scary when you let go and move forward with what comes up. Pixar provides training for their staff in how the creative process works, and their culture is very communicative. They train all new employees in how the communication structure works and it helps them to understand the culture of the company quicker.

When they start what seems like an impossible project, the team trusts that there is a solution just around the corner. This trust creates a vibrant environment and fantastic movies.

"The art challenges the technology, and the technology inspires the art."
John Lasseter, Chief Creative Officer, Pixar Studios

At Pixar they use feedback as a creativity tool on a daily basis, and they remind each other to not take the feedback too personally. Feedback is the other person's point of view, not the whole truth. They are aiming to make it feel safe to give and receive an opinion — it's a two-way collaboration. All teams show the other team members their work on a daily basis. It opens up the communication and they learn from each other.

In this sort of transparent, creative process, nobody can hide what they're working on. Early sharing makes the teams more creative and they are bonding with each other. To show what they have done might feel uncomfortable at first, but when they know that the team will help and support them, they will get used to it quickly. [Harvard Business Review, Sept, 2008]

Pixar is a hugely successful company, and I'm sure we'll enjoy many more of their movies in the future.

When you're in the process of learning how creativity and innovation works, it's perfect to learn from all kinds of businesses and organisations. Your problems might look different on the surface, but you're likely to have many issues in common. Be open for learning. If it works well at Pixar studios, it will work for you too.

DIGITAL LEADERSHIP PRINCIPLES

- All organisations can use the creativity principles and start being creative.

- Identify your biggest supporters and share your ideas with them first.

- Take responsibility for your own creativity.

- Learn more about the idea development process.

- Make it a habit that you and your team give each other feedback on a regular basis.

- Explore technology and learn how you can use it.

- Be a social brand online.

- Become better at building and maintaining your business relationships.

- Be a visible leader online and share your knowledge and insights. If you are not a member of any professional online networks, join now!

- Listen to feedback and be coachable.

- Say yes to new ideas.

- Always be a student and learn new insights.

CHAPTER 07

ONLINE INFLUENCING

If we look back at advertising history 50 or 60 years ago, you could put up an advert about almost anything and people would buy it. Today we live in the world with too many products, too many services and too much information. We have become very picky with all the options around us.

TOO MUCH INFORMATION (TMI)

Many of us, me included, are suffering from the problem Too Much Information (TMI). We're saving ourselves by filtering the information that's thrown on us.

When we look at how things are shared and pushed on us in the digital world, we're much more likely to trust what our friends are saying, compared to traditional pushy advertising.

ADVERTISING VERSUS OUR FRIENDS' OPINIONS

According to Nielsen 90% of us trust recommendations from those known to us and 70% trust recommendations from strangers. Only 14% will trust in advertising. When you as a company or organisation can get your fans to share your products, offers and insights online with their friends, you're going to get credit for that.

Every time someone in a network is sharing something with anyone else, you're more likely to get and engage an audience following you. You're much more likely to raise your awareness.

If you're selling tickets to an event, you're much more likely to sell more tickets if your customers are talking about your event. You'll get more followers and fans if your customers tell others about your event.

DOES 'WHO SAID WHAT' MATTER?

Social media is not just about being social, sharing and giving away information. It is also about credibility and influencing people in your network.

If you compare it to how we live in our society, we're all more likely to listen to people we trust and respect. It's the same rule online. We're much more likely to listen to honest people who are sharing an opinion they truly stand for.

Sofie says: *"We all have an OBD—an Online Bullshit Detector. We can see immediately if anyone shares something online and doesn't mean it. You are better off showing who you are, with your flaws, and keep being authentic to your values."*

MEASURING INFLUENCE

Many tools have been developed to measure online influence; the most common ones are Klout.com and Kred.com. They score you as an individual on how influential you are in your online social media channels.

At the moment, the most influential person online in the world is Barack Obama, and Justin Bieber is also doing very well. In the UK, Stephen Fry is very influential online. They all have one thing in common; they have a Klout score which is between 90 and 99, 100 being the highest. As a general rule of thumb, if you have a Klout score over 50, you are highly influential.

Sofie says: *"If you're looking at who is a real influencer in your network, check their Klout and Kred score. If they have a high score, explore how you can work with them."*

BRAND MARKETING WITH THE HELP OF INFLUENCERS

Many big brands are looking at their customers' influence scores. They are looking at their Klout or their Kred score to see how many people this person has in their network and how many people they will influence.

If you're very influential, you're likely to get more offers from companies. Your friends and business contacts will be very grateful for your likes, comments and sharing their posts. They know that many others who trust you will see their brand.

One example is Virgin Atlantic. They tested the promotion of a new route by rewarding relevant influencers found through Klout with free airline tickets. The efforts resulted in coverage on blogs and news outlets such as CNN, in addition to an impressive amount of mentions on Twitter.

ASK THE RIGHT PEOPLE TO SHARE YOUR BRAND ONLINE

To ask specific individuals to share your brand online is a smart way of doing a marketing campaign. In the future, we're going to be even more interested in who is who, who is sharing what and who is influencing who. I'm sure we will look more into how we're connected online and there will be more smart tools invented that explain how we all are connected with each other. Search for LinkedIn maps and you can see a map of all your LinkedIn connections — very impressive. You will get a better picture of the people in your network and how the people in it are connected.

Look at the influential people you have in your network and see if they might be able to help you. Maybe they can help you to raise awareness about an event, about a product or about a service you deliver.

CAN YOU BECOME AN ONLINE INFLUENCER?

Do you feel comfortable influencing other people or not? Do you admire other leaders online? Could you also do it? The answer to the last question is yes. If you put some effort into learning what your network is interested in and how you build trust among your followers, you are going to rock! You can be a niche influencer, you can be a celebrity star influencer, and you can choose to influence your local community. With all the digital tools available, you can choose if you would like to influence with a blog, a Facebook page or group, podcasts, videos and so on. You can share your opinions and insights with people in an open forum or a closed forum. All opportunities are there right in front of you.

As humans we know what makes a good voice online and what makes us listen to someone. It's very similar to socialising at a party. Someone who is negative and has a limited and unfriendly sense of humour will not be the social butterfly that people would like to talk to.

ANNOYING ONLINE VOICE	GREAT ONLINE VOICE
Same kind of message repeated all the time	Interesting and inspiring message
Send messages that make no sense in the context. No feeling for what makes people tick	You feel uplifted when you read or listen to their message
Total lack of humour	Interacting with their network, listens and replies
Are pushy, unfriendly and judgmental to others	Sharing on a regular basis. This becomes the rhythm that the audience gets used to
Negative messages and complaining a lot	Are generous with compliments to the members of their network
No interaction with their audience	Comment on what's going on in the world around them
Are trying to be someone they are not	Are honest about who they are and what they stand for

DIGITAL LEADERSHIP PRINCIPLES

- Find out who the influencers are in your network

- Know your own Klout or Kred score

- Ask the biggest influencers in your network if they would like to share your content and ideas with their network.

CHAPTER 08

WHAT YOU SHOULD AVOID DOING IN SOCIAL MEDIA

- Don't be a parrot repeating the same message. One-way communication will never sell you or your services.

- Never try to be someone who you are not. People will feel that there is something wrong with your online profile.

- Don't make mean comments about other people online. These comments might stay online forever. Do you remember what happened to HMV's Twitter feed? They deleted the tweets about 60 people being made redundant, but they will be available online forever as saved screen shots.

- Don't be inconsistent in your online profile picture. It should be obvious that it is you on Facebook, LinkedIn and Twitter etc.

- Never use an online profile photo that is a picture of a dog, cat or child. Show a photo of yourself. You have to show who you are online to be able to connect with other people.

- Never bombard your audience with too many sales messages. These messages tend to disengage your audience.

- Don't tag 50 of your friends in a photo so it will show up on their wall on Facebook or in a similar network. That is a way of spamming them.

You are likely to make mistakes online. If you say something inappropriate, you have to apologise, delete it and move on. You have to take action quickly; you can't wait for days and hope that people will listen to you then. Do it as early as you can.

If you are managing a team and you are using social media, the best way to avoid mishaps is training in what you can do. You should also provide training for everybody in the team in how your voice should be heard online. These actions are a good way to prevent future mistakes.

Sofie says: *"Be aware of what you post online. The digital shadow will stay with you even if you delete it. Your tweets, blogs and Facebook updates are likely to be stored somewhere online forever, as a screen shot or on a server."*

CHAPTER 09

CEOS AND BUSINESS EXECUTIVES SHOULDN'T FEAR DIGITAL MEDIA

Connect, tweet and click. Social media is fast, and if you're using a platform such as Twitter, you're getting exposed to the whole world and people can reply back to you immediately. There are no walls protecting you; you are potentially exposed to the whole world. It does take up some time, and you have to learn about online networking. Gosh, who has time for that? Isn't this just another critical risk? Social media and online networking does take a bit of time every day. And of course if you share inappropriate things online, there is risk involved, just as it would be with sending emails with sensitive content to everyone in your address book.

Former Medtronic Inc. CEO Bill George, a management professor at Harvard Business School and avid tweeter says: 'Most CEOs should accept that social media is part of their job description. People want CEOs who are real. They want to know what you think ... Can you think of a more cost-effective way of getting to your customers and employees?' [Wall Street Journal 26.9.2012]

At the moment very few CEOs and business executives are active in social networks. If you're a numbers person, you will love this: there are over 1 billion people on Facebook, over 500 million accounts on Twitter and research by Domo and CEO.com shows that only 7.6% of Fortune 500 CEOs have bothered to jump on Facebook, and just 4% have opened Twitter accounts. It looks to me as if there are a few more customers to gain for Facebook and Twitter.

Sofie says: *"If you can meet the love of your life online, I think it's a no-brainer that you can meet great business contacts online as well."*

I also know that many CEOs haven't bothered to get a proper LinkedIn account. I once worked in a place where the CEO had a LinkedIn account with only three connections. It sent out a very anti-social message to all employees, who of course noticed this and made fun of him. As a leader today your online brand is very important. It says a lot about you — what you stand for and believe in. In one of my workshops we researched some major British brands such as Primark, British Airways and Aston Martin. We could not find the CEOs on either LinkedIn or on Twitter. What does that say about them? What kind of message is that sending out?

5 TOP TIPS FOR BUSINESS EXECUTIVES TO BOOST THEIR SOCIAL MEDIA VISIBILITY

· Get started. Social media will stay in our lives, and it's about networking and connecting online. Especially if you find yourself working in a C-Suite (CEO, CMO, CIO, CFO), you need to be seen as innovative and connected, not as someone who's still using a typewriter when you should be using an iPad. Accept that the change is here to stay and start learning how digital media works.

· Check out who is active and influential on social media in your organisation. You can use Klout or Kred to see who is making an impact online already. Highly influential people in social media can be very helpful for your organisation. If your organisation is lacking influencers, it's time to encourage people to start using social media. If there's no one in your company in that category, find them and hire them. It's worth it. You don't want to end up in administration and bust as HMV did.

· Be authentic. It's much better to do most of the updates in your social networks yourself. Do fewer updates, but let the message come from you. Other people might inspire you with ideas and that will help you to be better. When I read updates on a Twitter account, I can say in less than 30 seconds if it's the person behind the name of the account who's written the updates or if it's the PR department.

- Make sure you track the feedback you get from your customers. If your company doesn't have an online customer support who tracks what people say about you on Twitter and so on it might be a good idea to get one. This isn't just a new way to keep in touch with your customers; it's about being responsive and connecting with your fan base.

- Allow people to try out new ways of communication online. Setting up too many rules will put people off and they might end up doing nothing. Get the legal team together with the social media experts in your organisation to write a social media policy. Things are moving swiftly in the social media world and policy needs to be updated on a regular basis. Proper training in what you're allowed to do in social media networks is the best prescription to avoid future mistakes.

If you have a leadership position in an organisation you need to support innovation and creativity. When you're using social media to communicate with your stakeholders, you'll be seen as an innovative leader. What we see today in social media is just the beginning, there is much more to come around the corner. Remember, everyone who posts online is a publisher. In a minute you can make your voice heard and inform and inspire others.

Learn from the best and check out Richard Branson's Twitter account. He has over 3 million followers. www.twitter.com/richardbranson

10 25 TIPS TO PROMOTE YOUR WEBSITE AND GROW YOUR ONLINE BRAND

You can use many techniques to promote yourself and your website online. Depending on your brand, your audience and message, you can use different tools and channels to reach out.

There are two rules that are crucial in every technique. The first one is good writing. Great copywriters rewrite the headlines and the way they describe their products or services several times. The headline is the attention grabber that will trigger your website visitors to read more and explore your site.

Rule number two is about the three Es:

1. **Engage**
2. **Entertain**
3. **Educate**

As a content creator you need to consider what your audience would like to read and listen to. What will keep them reading and listening, what will they find fun and what skill gaps do you need to fill?

Here I have collected 25 ways to promote yourself online and share what you or your business is up to.

1. Remind customers about your website address and social media channels on your products

Yes, remind your clients how to get in touch online. Easy and should be on more products.

2. Put your website address and social media channels on all your printed material

On your brochures, postcards and other paper products. Online and print works well together.

3. Always add your website address, social networks and events in your email footer

Whenever anyone from your organisation is sending an email, this will be seen in the footer.

4. Adverts online and pop-up window

Have you ever clicked on a pop-up window? For me this is a bit old-fashioned. I wouldn't recommend pop-up windows for any of my clients, but they are still used so apparently they still work.

5. Search engine optimisation (SEO)

Be found when someone is Googling your products and services. Super important!

6. Pay Per Click (PPC)

Buy ads from Google. This can cost a lot of money if not managed in a good way.

7. Email marketing

Build a great database of contacts and send updates about what's going on with your offers.

8. Automatic email programmes

This is very common. You get your audience to sign up and then you get them into an automatic email campaign.

9. Free downloads — ask website visitors to give you their email address

A great way to build your database is to give your visitors freebies.

10. Event marketing

Putting on the right kind of events can raise your brand online a lot! People are sharing the event with their friends and they will tweet and Facebook during the event.

11. Social media such as Facebook and Twitter

I think these two social networks are the foundation in most social media campaigns. You can also try out other social networks depending on where your audience is hanging out.

12. Start a blog and get the content to be shared in all kind of networks

Blogging about the kind of problems that your clients are having will boost your online brand. You'll be seen as an expert and authority.

13. Get a profile on image websites such as Instagram, Flickr and Pinterest

People love images and photos. Share them with others. And get your fans to share yours.

14. Membership /online communities

We love to feel special and to be invited to a group. Online there are many ways to communicate with your fans and also get them to get to know each other.

15. Online testimonials and reviews from customers

We're very likely to read online reviews before we make a decision about what to buy or where to go. Make sure your happy customers write a testimonial and that they share it in several online forums.

16. Online games

These are very popular. Loads of people want a fun game to play online.

17. Coupons / promotional codes / online vouchers / Groupon

Make special offers available to your clients that will save them money. Who doesn't like this?

18. Online competitions

We all want to win something. Be creative and engage your audience. Check out Facebook where there are always many competitions.

19. Podcasts

Podcasts are very good to offer as a download because your audience can listen to it when they have time. You can upload your content to online clouds; two of them are Mixcloud and SoundCloud.

20. Videos

YouTube is going to be even bigger in the future. Right now we're watching over 4 billion videos per day!

21. Build a mobile App

Who can live without their Smartphone and Apps? This is a very good way to share your online content and engage your customers.

22. QR codes

I'm not sure about how efficient they are at the moment. But I believe they will be used more in the future.

23. Online press releases

Publish a story about your business and post it online.

24. Become a guest blogger and link back to your website

If you share your knowledge on another blog, they will link back to your website as a thank you. Very efficient and you'll be seen as an expert in your field.

25. Speak about your business at different events

If you have the opportunity to speak about your business, take it. The audience will listen to you and you can share some of the problems you're solving for your customers and where they can find you online. Hand out your business cards to people who want to learn more.

HOW TO CHOOSE WHICH EGGS TO PUT IN THE BASKET

You can do a lot both offline and online to build your brand, and depending on your size and number of staff, you have to decide which eggs to put in your basket. Which are the digital techniques you would like to use to spread your brand? What comes naturally to you?

I always try to understand who my audience is and how they would like to be communicated with. What kind of message is right to send out? What kind of message will the audience connect with? When I'm preparing a speech or a blog post, I'm considering who will listen to this message and what kind of words, expressions and stories are they likely to connect with?

One more important aspect is your own energy. What feels most natural and fun to you? Are you a natural networker who loves to go to events or are you better at managing an online club? Do you love writing blog posts?

If you feel like setting up an online community such as a Facebook group or LinkedIn group, you will be more influential if you keep it small and personal. If you have a group with 50 members, you can influence most of them with one post. If your community has 10,000 members, you will influence more, but the members might not feel connected to you on a personal level.

When managing a team or a business, you need to find people who have a mixture of skills. I believe we all have different talents and when putting together a digital team you need to combine different abilities and experiences. If you have the right mix of people in your team, you're going to reach out in most channels using videos, podcasts, blog posts, email newsletters and social media, and you're going to use a message that connects with your customers.

To put together and manage a good digital team takes time and effort. By using the creativity principles I am teaching, you're going to make the most out of each person's abilities.

Sofie says: *"We go online to connect with others and we connect with people we want to do business with. The deeper connection, the more money we're likely to spend. We trust tips we get from friends and we read online testimonials. They are all guiding us in our buying decisions. If people trust you, they are more likely to spend money on your services and you can only build trust by genuinely connecting."*

11 HOW CAN YOU BECOME A DIGITAL LEADER?

Words are indeed powerful. Words are creating the stories that are told by people all over the world. We are still telling tales from ancient Greek mythology and we are interpreting Shakespeare's dramas in hundreds of different ways and styles. We do this because even the old stories are inspiring us to think about our lives differently. They help us to see how the world works from new perspectives.

If you are aspiring to become a creative digital leader, your words will be one of the best tools you have available. They will inspire many people, whether written or spoken.

You have many options for how you can use your voice online — how you can become a digital leader. You can start a blog, create videos, tweet, add photos on Instagram, update your Facebook status and make it public, or set up a Facebook page. I believe that one of the most effective ways to create power and influence others is by starting a blog. A blog is like an online book where you can write about your life, your experiences, your thoughts and your ideas.

A person who blogs can have a huge impact on their colleagues, customers and the world around them. They are communicating their thoughts and ideas to the whole world and that opens up all kind of conversations and development. I have collected some blogs written by CEOs, which can be found on the link below. Please note that I'm not endorsing any of the brands, CEOs or the content in the blogs.

CEO who blogs www.sofiesandell.com/2013/01/31/blogging-ceos

DIGITAL TOOLS YOU CAN USE FOR BECOMING A LEADER ONLINE

The foundation is to have good content, and then you publish it in one place online, it might be your blog. The next step is to share it in your online social media networks.

Popular social media networks

Facebook — you can use your own page, fan page
                    or start a group
Twitter   — have your say in 140 characters
LinkedIn   — set up your own profile and start groups
Google+   — set up your own profile and
                    join communities.

Blogging tools

Blogger
WordPress
Tumblr

Image tools

Instagram
Pinterest
Flickr

Online video

YouTube
Vimeo

You can coordinate your updates and posts with the help of tools such as Hootsuite.

BASIC STEPS TO BECOMING A LEADER ONLINE

If you don't know where to start your digital adventure, here are some tips that will help you to get started. Thousands of people have already done it, so now you can do it too. If you would like to share more of your thoughts, start and set up a blog and website. You can use free tools to do this; WordPress, Blogger and Tumblr are three of the biggest content management systems you can use.

Update your online profiles and make sure you are sending out a similar message in your online networks. LinkedIn is more professional; Facebook has a more friendly touch. Be active on Twitter if you feel that short, impactful messages work for you. People that find you online should see that it's you on all networks that you've joined; so don't be an expert on dogs in one network and then an expert in technology in another. Combine your personality and skills and tell the world what you do and how you can help.

Start connecting with your network using LinkedIn. Go through your business cards you have collected over the years and send a friendly contact request to the people you met. Connect with your colleagues and ex-colleagues. LinkedIn is a great tool to use to connect with your network from school and university. People are on different paths in their lives and it's great to know a bit more about what they are up to.

In the last 12 months, I have noticed that the people you meet are more open to immediately connect on Facebook. In the past I always added new acquaintances on LinkedIn, but now this seems to have changed and new people are more open to add me on Facebook. If you feel this works for you, you can send people you just met a Facebook request. It is up to you if you feel that it is appropriate to add new contacts in your Facebook network or if you only what to keep that for people you know more personally.

When you attend events, it's common that they use a #hashtag, which is a word or phrase prefixed with the hash symbol that people use on social networking services to connect. It can be a brand name or event and date such as #London2012. Then you can connect with the other attendees, both those who are at the live event and those who are online. It's easy to search for a hashtag on Twitter.

One of the best functions with LinkedIn is the groups. You can join up to 50 groups and you can start a discussion and also contribute to the discussions.

All online networks follow the same social rules. If you contribute to the network sharing your thoughts and ideas in a nice and friendly way, people will like you. However, if you are not sharing anything at all, people will not notice you. If you are repeating the same message over and over again, the network will stop listening to you. Always have in mind 'Am I contributing to the network in any way by adding this message online?'

Sofie says: *"Engage, entertain and educate your network and they will see you as a leader who they want to listen to."*

12 TIPS TO CREATE GREAT BLOG CONTENT TO GENERATE INTEREST AND SALES

A few years ago it was trendy to start blogging. People were blogging about everything between heaven and earth without having any kind of content strategy behind it. Many of the blogs died due to lack of content. To avoid the trap of running out of content, I'm sharing some tips with you.

There are millions of blogs out there trying to reach an audience. When you start your blog, it will take a few posts before you 'find your voice'. Some people find it daunting to suddenly be a publisher and that the whole world is going to scrutinize your posts. Yes, you're visible all over the world and many of your clients will read what you wrote. Should you worry? I would say as long as you share an experience or something engaging or educational you're safe. It's when you're starting to share irrelevant facts that nobody reads that you should consider getting someone to help you out.

So how do you write a post that people will read and share? You might be thinking first *What do I write about?* Here are a few tips for where to get ideas for online content.

TIPS FOR CONTENT

- **Problems**

Consider what concerns your clients have; what are they asking you about? Then write a blog post that solves their problems.

- **Industry topics & timing**

Be among the first to comment on a topic you know is being discussed in your industry then share it with everyone in your network. People will link to your post and share it with their network.

- **Be personal — be real**

Write about one of your recent experiences, good or bad. Mention a person you met who helped you to solve a problem. It shows that you're appreciating people who help you!

- **Make comments**

Read other people's blogs and make a comment if you like the article or comment if you disagree. You will find lots of inspiration from reading other people's blog posts.

- **YouTube**

Search for what others are saying on YouTube about your areas of interest. Play with what they are communicating in the video, add your own view and voila; you have new content for a blog post!

- **Interviews**

Interview a person who you admire and find inspiring online. Publish it on your blog. Ask if they would like to share your interview with their network. You're getting free promotion.

You can write long or short posts. Use inspiring images. Add a video. Write 'Best of' lists and 'Top Tips' lists. There are many different ways to share your insights, knowledge and experience.

ONLINE COPYWRITING CHECKLIST

So what if you're selling something, maybe a product, service or event? There are a few rules that will make people read your post, and if they like what they read, they will buy from you.

- **Main point**

Make the main point the main point. Make sure that your main point stands out. Include the most exciting benefits in the first five sentences. Then your readers are more likely to read the rest of your message.

- **Make it scannable to the eye**

Break up the content. Short paragraphs are easier for readers to quickly scan and you're always striving for making your content scannable as people are always short on time and have short attention spans.

- **Headlines**

Focus a lot of effort into getting the headlines right. That's one of the key converters in your blog. Bad headline = no readers. When your customers see a compelling and inspiring headline, they will read the rest.

- **Readability test**

A readability test is one of the best kept secrets for great copywriting. I often check that my copy is following the best practise for plain English. There is a free online service that will do this for you: www. online-utility.org. You can also check your text in Microsoft word.

You should try to have under sixteen words per sentence when writing online. Flesch Reading Ease around 60 indicates that it's written in plain English.

Sofie says: *"Always get the basics right when you are sharing your message online. Learn from other online influencers and be open to feedback."*

If you feel insecure about a text and can't figure out what's wrong with it, it can be worth checking the readability. If it's low you know why you find it hard to read.

PART THREE

MASTERING THE CREATIVE FLOW

"You can't use up creativity. The more you use, the more you have."

Maya Angelou

CHAPTER 13

13 WAKING UP THE INNOVATIVE SPIRIT
- YOUR PERSONAL CREATIVITY

Creativity starts within you and in this chapter I am going to explain further what creativity is. We were all born with the gift to be creative; it was there inside us from the start. Unfortunately, as children grow and progress through school, much of this natural creativity is squashed. I remember school as being very task-oriented. If you were the first to finish your work, you were seen as a star, and you would sometimes be rewarded. There was comparison and competition going on, and we were always striving for something better — but better in the A to B way the teacher wanted, not better in a more creative way.

This way of studying and learning worked well for some students — those who were always encouraged when they performed well and according to what the teacher told us. But it was detrimental for the students who didn't work as quickly. I often wanted to try a different route and this made me a bit slower. Some teachers got upset with students who experimented. I was one of these 'do it my way' students. In the end I learnt a lot, but my self-confidence was damaged and it did take time to understand that it was okay to do things the way that worked for me.

When we enter work-life as adults after many years in school environments, we're expected to be creative again. It can take some time and effort to get the creative flow moving again, as it did for me. If you feel a bit hesitant and unsure if you can be creative or not, I would like to assure you that EVERYONE can be creative! If anyone tells you differently, they don't know what they are talking about. I've been studying creativity for many years, and it's been established by creativity experts that everyone has creative abilities. So if anyone tells you you're not creative, ask them to do the research themselves. Or maybe they're just not very creative themselves and can't see beyond the end of their own nose.

When you're in your creative state of mind, don't be afraid of the 'bad' ideas that come up. They will eventually lead you to the useful ideas. You can't tell, initially, if an idea is good or bad. Often, from the craziest, most outrageous ideas spring the most beautiful inspirations. Your idea might be an ugly duckling that just needs to find its new friends.

WHAT'S STOPPING CREATIVE IDEAS TO COME ALIVE?

Company history, legacy and culture combined with people's behaviour will determine how successful and creative the organisation will be. In many organisations today, there are internal politics going on that prevent employees from expressing themselves and fully utilising their creative talent. It affects everyone in the company. Often individuals feel stressed, and there's no tolerance for creativity or innovation, and as a result this makes the employees even more inefficient.

If you want a successful, creative and innovative organisation, you want everyone in your team to feel empowered. All contributors should feel that they are free to share their ideas with others. Aim to create a culture where creativity is encouraged and ideas can grow. It is very similar to gardening. You plant a seed and give it water and sunshine. Screaming at the plant, and demanding that it grow, will not do any good. (Actually a lot of people believe plants grow better with classical music, so I'm quite sure screaming at plants doesn't help at all.) It won't grow faster because you want it to. But if you're providing a nourishing environment, and allow the plant to thrive, you'll be rewarded with a beautiful flower. People work exactly the same way. If they are nurtured, they will yield great results.

DARE TO FAIL

One of the best ways to learn how to be creative is by making mistakes. I've made lots of mistakes when I've been working with digital media, and while leading others. I've learnt a lot and I've also shared my knowledge and experience with others.

A good basic recipe is to do one mistake per week. This will keep you on your toes and you'll learn new things and see new approaches for your work. The companies that are in the Teenage category all have made many mistakes, and they are still keen to explore what they can do and what's next. They just pick themselves up, dust themselves off and try the next big idea.

Some of the biggest creative people in history produced thousands of ideas and most of them were below average — and some of them made them world famous. They allowed themselves to fail and make mistakes. Mozart produced over 600 pieces of music — most of them we are not familiar with. Shakespeare wrote 154 sonnets, and some of them are brilliant, some bad and some just average. They allowed themselves to create over the whole span from bad to brilliant. You can do this too.

*"Everyone has talent. What is rare
is the courage to follow the talent to the
dark place where it leads."*
Erica Jong

To be able to open up your creative flow you have to find out what's inspiring you. You're unique in your own way; discover what makes you tick. We all feel inspired by different activities and things. The inspiration you are looking for doesn't normally fall down from the sky; you have to go out and chase it. If I have a period when I don't do what I enjoy, my creative spirit dies a bit.

I often act as a creativity doctor when people are feeling stuck. We identify what some of their problems are and what they need to do. It's similar to coaching. I simply look at what you need to do more of in your life to flourish more often. When you have recently done something you love, your mind works much better.

Sarah, a client of mine, was feeling stuck in her job and at the same time she stopped playing golf, one of her favourite sports. When she didn't do what she loved doing — her golf — her mind got even more stuck, and in the end it was impossible for her to find a solution to her problems. After a couple of months mostly spent working, she took a day off and went to the golf course. The next week she changed her work situation and got involved in tasks that inspired her.

Sofie says: *"You have to go out and chase your own creativity. Your creativity won't sit in front of you in the morning asking you to work together."*

HOW TO MANAGE THE FLOW OF YOUR IDEAS

I believe innovation and creativity starts within you. Here I am sharing some of my thoughts to help you boost your own creative abilities.

Ideas come and go. Get a scrap book and write them down or maybe use an online spreadsheet if that is better for you. Most importantly, collect them in one place, not random pieces of paper that you keep everywhere. Joanna, who runs her own business, uses an audio recorder, and every evening before she goes to bed she records a summary of the ideas she has in her head. She then listens to them on her way into work the next day. Her husband thinks she is a bit crazy, but this is a method that works for her.

Leonardo da Vinci was obsessed with keeping fit; he knew it was crucial for his creativity to look after his body. The body, mind and spirit are connected. Give them new energy and they will work better together. Going out for a walk or exercise is a creativity trick that works for most of us. Moving your body is one of the best ways to stop feeling stuck. Every time I finish a workout session I find myself solving a lot of problems — I get super creative. Everything that seemed impossible during the day becomes so easy when I'm doing some exercise. For me it seems I get very creative when I do sit-ups. I've been fascinated by this for years and I didn't have a clue why it works until recently when I read about it in an article. Your body is creating a special protein when you're exercising called 'brain-derived neurotrophic factor' (BDNF), and this is a fertilizer for the brain.

BDNF helps the brain to build more connections. It also makes your current connections between neurones and synapses stronger. It's these connections that are creating new patterns, and new patterns and paths means that we see things differently. A walk is free. It only costs you the time you're investing and it is a great way to nurture your creativity and ideas. This means that if you have a problem at work, you should go for a walk. Or you should ask your boss if it is okay to get a treadmill for the office. You can pick up a lot from books, seminars, TV and discussions; they open up your mind to new possibilities. Become a lifelong learner.

Be ambitious and set up seemingly impossible goals. This will help you to start looking for new solutions both unconsciously and with your conscious mind. Think about Larry Page and Sergey Brin who founded Google. They wanted to organise all information on the web and make it accessible for everyone. That's a very ambitious goal. If you let the goal fertilise in your brain for a while, you will find solutions to even the most impossible goal.

Improve all the communication channels around you. It helps if you can talk and communicate with others when you're developing your ideas. When Will McInnes wrote his book Culture Shock he added each new chapter on a blog and asked for feedback. This helped him to develop the content and it was open for anyone to comment.

Get support from some very positive people. We all need encouragement when being creative and innovative. Get rid of the people who want to take you down to their own low level. Many times it has been the small encouraging words that have changed my view of the world. Last year I went to a party and everyone I met gave me loads of positive feedback about my projects, ideas and my personality. The next month was my most efficient month ever and this was thanks to the compliments. We love to hear another human being's voice telling us positive things about how amazing we are. A positive comment is free; it costs you nothing.

Innovation is not necessarily an invention. If an inventor discovers the next big thing but is unable to find anyone to deliver it as a product or service then the next big thing remains undiscovered to the world. That is not innovation.

Sofie says: *"Innovation has to be spread and used by others. If not, it remains a secret and secrets won't change the world."*

All organisations need to work on improvements all the time. It's from here that many innovations will appear. Naturally, we are continually working on improvement and sometimes we're doing it consciously, which can be very effective. We need to think: 'What is the next big thing?' Open up our imagination and start picturing a better future in our mind. If you open up the creative collective consciousness in your group, you will achieve great results.

Do the exercise *Setting Your Conditions for Creativity* in chapter 21 every now and then. That will remind you about what you need to do to be creative. I don't think it is an easy task to find your own inner creativity, but you have to try to find it every day. When you have done that a few times, it will come easier to you and you'll get into your creative mood quicker.

DARE TO ASK FOR FEEDBACK

Creativity is about being precise, about centimetres and inches. Invite the people around you to fine-tune your offers. It doesn't have to be perfect to start with, but ask for feedback and it will improve a lot. When I've been working on any project, it's always valuable feedback from others that helps me create a better product or service. By using the creativity principles you will get better at giving feedback and you will be more conscious when you listen to feedback.

Have you ever visited an Apple store and been welcomed by the happy employees? If not, I can tell you that the staff there are very helpful, chatty and friendly. I spoke to Felix who's working in one of the Apple stores. He said that they have created a system and culture in which feedback is given by everyone to everyone. 'You just ask your colleague if he or she is open for feedback, and then you tell him or her what can be done in a better way.' To give and receive feedback is part of their jobs. As Brian Tracy famously said, 'Feedback is the breakfast of champions'- something that Apple stores are all too aware of.

A true feedback champion is David Copperfield, the illusionists. He overcame his shyness with doing magic tricks, and every time he did a trick he asked for feedback. This made him progress and at the age of sixteen David was an adjunct professor at New York University where he taught a course called The Art of Magic. David is one of the most famous illusionists in the world and he is still learning new illusions, always pushing himself and his team members forward.

When you ask for feedback, you may feel hurt and misunderstood. This is common and the person telling you their opinion may not be aware they are hurting you. If you work on your mental armour shield and make that stronger, you will feel less hurt the next time. It's only the other person's opinion, not the whole truth. For me it helps to think that they are criticising the idea, not me.

Some of the world's most famous geniuses were judged by others, and they continued to believe they were on the right track:

· According to one professor Einstein was 'the laziest dog' the university ever had.

· The parents of Beethoven were told that their son was too stupid to become a music composer.

· In the beginning of his career Walt Disney was told he lacked imagination.

None of the claims above were true. It was just that person's opinion, which they expressed by judging Einstein, Beethoven and Walt Disney.

LACK OF MONEY CAN MAKE YOU PROSPER

One of the most common excuses for people to not take action is that they don't have any money. But lack of large budgets can create amazing solutions. New partnerships are born; organisations that could never imagine working together are now collaborating. It's our method of approaching problems that makes us think in a new direction. This is where creativity is vital.

Many of my friends in Junior Chamber International UK participated in a project called £1 per day challenge in 2013. The whole point was to live off £1 per day during one week. It might sound impossible at first, but there were over 30 people participating and they managed to do it. The project got attention online and it was mentioned by many influential people on Twitter.

The project made it easy to build relationships and get others involved. One of the biggest lessons for the people who participated was that they were looking at their life from a new perspective and they learnt how to avoid wasting food. A project with zero budget and small running cost made an impact. All the money that the participants would have used for food during the week was donated to Save the Children.

DIGITAL OPPORTUNITIES ARE EVERYWHERE

Yes, you have the internet available 24 hours per day and you can create amazing projects and involve thousands of people directly.

In my projects I've often worked with someone on the other side of the world. Cherry who designed the images in this book lives in the Philippines and I chose her because I liked her style. I looked at many other designers' work, but it was with her I clicked. The project went very smoothly and it didn't matter that she was in another time zone.

CAN YOU BE CREATIVE?

Nobody said it was easy to be creative. We're brought up in a society where we're rewarded for being critical and finding problems. Another common behaviour is predicting the outcomes if you perform a task a certain way. This behaviour is one of the bigger issues we have in organisations today. Painting the devil on the wall before you start doesn't give anyone positive energy.

The most innovative companies are staying in a creative life stage when developing and they have created an environment where they can nurture an idea and make it grow into something bigger. It takes hard work to get this cultural behaviour working. People who are predicting a disaster or telling their colleagues that their ideas are bad need to be reprogrammed. These people are creativity killers and will never be digital leaders if they do not change their behaviour.

Sofie says: *The good thing about creativity*
            is that it is a behaviour that can
            be learnt.

I once worked in an anti-creative organisation where people were blaming each other for all kinds of things. The organisation was not successful and had big problems with cash flow. If you would like to encourage creativity, you have to stop the blame game. That will not lead to prosperity. A blame game culture won't create the opportunities you need in order to get more clients.

> *"Positive thinking takes courage.*
> *Negative thinking takes nothing."*
> **Sofie Sandell**

The first step to changing your circumstances is to stop blaming somebody else for what's happening in your life and with your job. Does it sound familiar? We have all tried to blame our friends, colleagues and family for what is happening in our lives and careers.

We all know people who are blaming EVERYTHING on other people. Doing that means they give away their power to do something about their lives. Just because you feel you're stuck doesn't mean that's the case. Thoughts come and go, and negative thoughts will go away if you choose to focus on how you can change the situation.

Creativity will lead to more creativity and this will lead to higher profit and new opportunities. The world doesn't need more average solutions. We need extraordinary and great solutions to change the world.

We need people to work creatively together to find new and great solutions. This is valid for most projects, and if you're aware of the digital opportunities you will incorporate them into your solutions.

CREATIVITY PRINCIPLES IN PRACTICE

This is a story about Jeroen Komen founder of Knoworries in the Netherlands and how, by thinking creatively, he set up his business and travelled the world.

'As an 18 year old I hitchhiked from Holland to Jerusalem. Arriving with only $10 left and no return ticket I quickly found a job as a dishwasher in a 4-star hotel and stayed in a youth hostel that normally cost $5 per day. I made friends with the lady from the hotel laundry who offered to do my clothes as well. She asked about the leftovers from the dishwashing as she wanted them to feed her cats. I ended up scooping them into plastic bags and giving them to the laundry lady. She in return gave me the hotel sheets that had cigarette burns on them. No good for a 4-star hotel, fine for the youth hostel I stayed in. For every sheet I got a free night of accommodation.

Then I went on a 3-day trip to Egypt where I bought 300 packages of cigarette papers. They were heavily taxed in Israel, so after I sold them I had enough money to fly to London. From there I hitchhiked back home.

Some years later I hitchhiked to a job fair in Amsterdam. The gentleman who gave me a ride hired me some weeks later to set up IT facilities in his company. Five years later, this company was the first customer of my company Knoworries. Some years later I had 10+ employees.

One of my employees didn't quite fit the changes that came with a growing company. It would have been wise for him to find a job elsewhere. Almost a year after assessments and coaching and good intentions, he still hadn't resigned. Quite a difficult situation for an employer, but then he and I discovered that he didn't really want another job; he'd much rather go traveling. There we found a mutual passion. I bought him an airline ticket to Bangkok and he resigned. We're still good friends.

At some stage my company could run well without me, so I formalized that. With all the free time I improved my hobby as a photographer. I also bought a small, home-built plane and decided to fly to the Montreux Jazz Festival with it. Passe-partout tickets there were very expensive. I registered as a photographer, giving my photos to a Dutch Jazz Magazine for free. With the press pass I could see many concerts from the first rows. And during the festival I stayed with a wonderful host family that I had found through couchsurfing.org.

During the festival, I took photos of a Tatarian model who turned out to also be the director of the kick-off day of St. Gallen Business University. She hired me as a keynote speaker to inspire young students to think differently about earning more money. When I've been building relationships with the people I met, there are two online networks that have been helping me, Couchsurfing and LinkedIn. Both are door openers and they have helped me to build relationships that I would never have had if not connecting online first.'

CREATIVE LEADERSHIP PRINCIPLES

· Everyone can be creative.

· Find out what inspires you and do these things often.

· Get a single book to write down all your ideas, or keep them online in Google drive.

· Keep your body fit, go for a walk if you're stuck.

· Read books, listen to speeches and always broaden your knowledge.

· Set ambitious goals.

· Improve your communication channels.

· Get a group of supportive people around you.

14 OUR AMAZING BRAIN

Don't you love your brain? It's always with you, and the way you use it is a big part of your personality. This is a quick lesson about how our brain works and how it's helping us in our daily lives.

In our brain we have millions of connections made up by neurones. Where the neurones meet we have a synapse that is joining the paths. Every thought you have is travelling through a neurone and its travelling super-fast. It is in these neurones and synapse connections that we are creating our thought patterns.

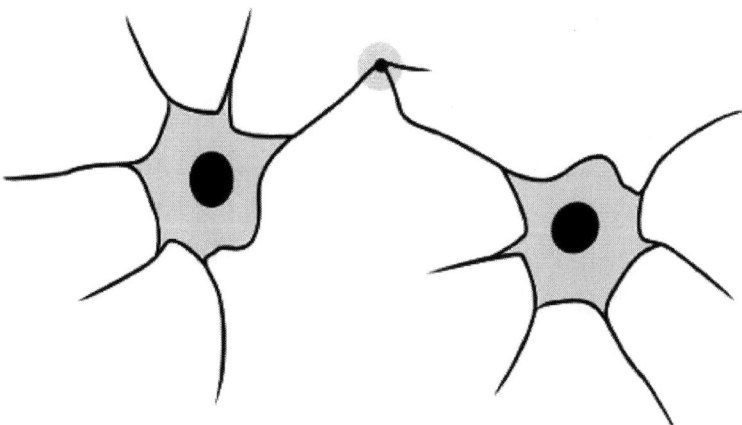

Two neurones meet via a synapse

The more often you have a thought, the deeper the connection and pattern is made in your brain. And the more often you're repeating something the deeper imprinted it will become. Just like a trail that turns into a track. One pair of feet leaves almost no trail on the ground, but when many pairs of feet follow the same road, they will leave a strong track, and in the end it will be a highway. It's the same with your thoughts. Imagine what this means for negative thoughts. When a negative thought follows another, it makes it even easier for the third to find its way. Don't you think it's about time to stop allowing negative thoughts to shape your brain?

Every day we have thousands of thoughts going through our head. Brain experts are saying that we have between 60–80,000 thoughts going through our brain every single day.

I would like to ask you a question:
'How many of the 60–80,000 thoughts you have every day are you aware of, and how many are you not aware of?'

Many things we're doing in our daily lives are what we learnt when we were very young. Things that would be very time consuming and annoying to do in a conscious state if we had to. Imagine if you had to think consciously every time you were: eating breakfast, talking to family members, having a shower, reading a book, taking the bus, cycling. It's great that our brain has created a pattern for us here and that we don't have to think when we're doing them. Other situations when you must have access to these patterns are in dangerous situations. We know that we should not walk on the motorway and we are also aware that an iron can be hot and you get burned if you touch it. These are great warning patterns and save us from injuries.

But some of the patterns we have created are not helping us to be creative. We get stuck in our own thought patterns about how the world works and what's possible. This is often called having 'limiting beliefs', and the more we work on them the better we will be at breaking them.

One of the most famous examples of limiting beliefs is the 'four minute barrier'. Nobody thought it was possible to run one mile (1,609 meters) in under four minutes. In 1954 Roger Bannister ran the mile in

3:59:4 minutes and many runners have done it since. Now it's the standard of all male professional middle distance runners. It took one person to show it was possible and the rest followed.

Our conscious mind is working when we're doing something for the first time. I remember when I was learning how to drive a car. In the beginning it was impossible for me to talk and drive at the same time. All my concentration went into driving the car. Now many years later there is no problem with driving and talking at the same time, I've created a pattern in my brain and I do many of the movements without any conscious thinking.

In my daily life I'm in my cosy comfort zone most of the day. Every now and then I'm a bit lost and I'm creating a new pattern in my brain. The first time I meet a new person I am to work with, I'm learning about them and I'm getting to know how their business works. This is an example of creating a new thought pattern.

When I'm lost and don't know where I'm going, I'm creating a new learning pattern about how to find my way. There is a saying that I've heard: 'never trust anyone who's never been lost.' You will probably get more inspiring tips from a person who has been exploring while being lost than from someone who has explored the world with a precise map.

When you are learning a new sport, you are using your conscious mind. After a while you start to see patterns and you understand the rules. I once met Peter in a workshop and he told me how his football team had developed a common thought pattern and now they only have to look at each other to understand what's next. This kind of common knowledge and consciousness appears when you have great connection and understanding between the team members. Peter described it as magic.

In 2012 I set a goal to train 100 people in how creativity works. I wrote it down in my note book. By the end of 2012 I had trained 100 people. When I had written this, I had no idea how I was going to do it, but somehow these 100 people turned up.

This year my goal is to train 1,000 people in digital leadership and how creativity works. I've no idea who they are yet. This is a way for me to challenge my thinking patterns and create new solutions. When you are setting a goal that feels too big, you are expanding your thoughts and you create a new pattern that will give you the solution you need.

*'If you put yourself in a position where
you have to stretch outside your comfort zone then
you're forced to expand your consciousness.'*
Les Brown

CAN YOU CHANGE A HABIT?

Have you ever tried to change another person's habit? Nagged them, saying that they have to change this or that? Did it work successfully? It's very likely that the person didn't change his or her behaviour at all. I would like to share one of my experiences when I changed one of my habits.

One of the bigger changes I've made in my life was to become a morning person. As long as I can remember I've always been an evening person who loves staying up late. The effect of this was that I was tired in the morning.

A few years ago I decided to break this pattern and my new personality was to become a morning person. My way of doing this was to exercise in the mornings. I found an outdoor bootcamp ten minutes away from where I live and they were meeting at 6.45 am, three days per week.

For the first four months I was terribly tired and I was yawning throughout all sessions. Then one day I didn't feel tired any longer. I had changed my pattern and forced myself to become more awake earlier. It took over 100 days to do this, and it's probably one of the biggest changes I've made so far.

To break a deep pattern around how you do something in your life can take a long time. Especially if they are as deeply rooted as mine was, being an evening person and not a morning person.

If your organisation is going through change, it may also take time. Don't expect everyone to buy into the idea in one go. We all have a different acceptance rhythm. Everyone has a different view of the world, and you have to allow people some time when changing something or trying out something new. Most people will accept change.

I once worked with a change consultant and she said that many senior executives are planning for the change for months and they have a perfect understanding of how well it will work after being involved in the process. When they present the change to the rest of the company, they get annoyed with the resistance they meet. She said: 'Are they expecting that everyone will love the change as soon they hear it, while the senior people presenting it had months to accept it?'

> "Resistance is not a peripheral opponent.
> It does not arise from rivals, bosses, spouses,
> children, terrorists, lobbyists, or political
> adversaries. It comes from us."
> **Steven Pressfield**

BREAK YOUR THOUGHT PATTERNS

When you're doing something for the first time, it may feel scary, it's daunting and you're hesitating. It's exactly how it felt for me the first time I was driving a car. After a while you get used to the activity and things are not scary or daunting any longer.

If you're going to innovate the way you approach your business you'll most likely feel the same. Doing something for the first time will make you feel nervous. And you might have heard negative comments along the way and they are still clanging around in your mind. This is normal and all big innovations and ideas that came true have gone through this stage.

If you and your colleagues are developing knowledge about how the brain is working and getting familiar with the idea process, you're going to be more successful when you need to break a thought pattern.

It will still feel scary, but when you've verbalised that you have to break patterns and discussed the idea process, you're going to open up a new world. The language you're using is going to change. You can almost say that you're learning a new language when learning how ideas and creativity works.

Sofie says: *"It won't help much if only a few people know the language of creativity. You need to give everyone in your organisation access to this amazing tool."*

CHAPTER 15

PROBLEM SOLVING IN DAILY WORK LIFE

When we're growing up and going to school, many of us are in a problem solving environment. It's about focusing on getting us from A to B in the easiest way. After years in education we are very problem-focused and we are used to being rewarded for our ability to solve a problem quickly. At work we often find ourselves feeling great when a problem has been solved and our colleagues are praising our ability to solve a problem. This habit of seeking reward for solving problems quickly may in fact jeopardise finding a long-lasting, creative solution. Let's look at the types of problems there are and the usual approach to fixing them, and how we could choose another route.

DIFFERENT KINDS OF PROBLEMS

- Small annoying issues
- Fire fighting problems — solve now or die
- Continual problems

Small annoying issues are things that can be solved by taking small actions. It can be a problem with your computer that a colleague is helping you with. Or it can be almost anything that will take 10 minutes or less to solve. You won't get much recognition by solving these small annoying issues.

The fire-fighter problems are urgent and have to be dealt with immediately, or your project might mess up totally. An example is that you must send a big order manually by driving yourself through town to an important client. The person that solved an emergency, fire-fighter problem will most likely get a pat on the back and recognition for being smart and action-oriented. Of course, their input was great; something had to be done. With our deep pattern from being problem-oriented during our school years, we are likely to aim for this kind of quick and fast recognition. It makes us feel great.

Many people are searching for the chance to show off by being a fire fighter. They love to calm down their colleagues by telling them the story of how they solved the problem. This kind of problem solving and approach, because it's done quickly on your feet, is not breaking any patterns and you're solving the problems with the same thinking patterns as you used many times before. There's a pitfall in this approach.

When a problem keeps coming up repetitively it's a continual problem. Often the approach is to set up a strategic meeting (even if only with oneself) in which we'll discuss the problem and how to approach it. I've been to plenty of strategic meetings and in some of them the problem is solved, but in many the main problem remains and comes back up again. Why? Because the solutions that are formulated are developed using current thinking patterns and these are only going to serve up something similar or familiar. You're not going to cook a delicious Mongolian meal if you're still using French recipes.

The best approach to problem solving is creative problem solving. In essence, you can say that this includes a path that you and your team have never taken before. To be able to dig into a problem like this you need to use creativity techniques such as the 'Yes, and...' creativity tools and games, and you need the trust to dare to try out new combinations.

When you do this, new patterns will come alive. You already have many answers in your amazing brain that are just waiting to be discovered, and together with the people you meet every day you can create new creative solutions.

CREATIVE PROBLEM SOLVING TECHNIQUES

You can use creative problem solving techniques in many ways, and I am going to give you a list of some techniques that I find helpful. Before you start, always define the problem as best you can, then everyone who is involved will have a better understanding and you are more likely to come up with a solution that everyone is happy with.

- Involve a random word or object in your discussion and the output has to involve the random word or object.

- Go for a walk and discuss the problem; new impressions will help you to see new angles and you get more creative when you are moving your body.

- Play improvisation and association games

- Brainstorm

- Combine two ideas — this can create a brilliant solution.

- Develop a crazy solution and peel off the craziness and get a new solution that fits your organisation.

- Have a discussion and everyone who is there has to say, 'Yes, that's brilliant' to all ideas. This creates amazing energy and is fun.

If you would like to learn more about the techniques, there are many free resources available online and you can buy books about the topic.

16 LEARN TO BE NICE TO IDEAS

In the beginning stages of idea and concept development, it's often impossible to see the difference between a great idea and a bad idea. They might have the same shape and form and express themselves in a similar way. You need to give them energy to grow before you judge the idea too quickly.

It's nice to be in your comfort zone, isn't it? But the risk is that you're repeating the same pattern. Another big risk is that you're not looking into new opportunities to build your business if you're hanging out in your comfort zone too much. When someone has a new idea and you have a feeling it won't work out, you might get this feeling because it is taking you far outside of where you normally are in your life.

This example shows how difficult it can be to see the difference between a bad and a great idea.

> 'I'm out having fun with my friends, and there is a man approaching me. I look at him and I judge him by the way he dresses, and I end the conversation after one minute. Later that evening a very handsome man speaks to me and I get very flattered by all his compliments. Who of these guys has the potential of being a great date? You can't tell because I didn't give the first guy a proper chance; I judged him too quickly. It's the same with new ideas; you need to evaluate them and let them expand a bit more before you say yes or no to them.'

To create an allowing environment you need to challenge your thought patterns. It's exhausting to start thinking differently, but if you would like to develop your creative skills it's necessary.

Sofie says: *"Be aware of your language. If you don't have any positive comments, resist saying anything when conducting the evaluation of an idea in its early stage. The 'Yes, and...' phrase tool are two of the most powerful words you can use."*

Wonderful ideas can look like a bad idea in the beginning so you need to work on it before it will turn into a great idea. Dare to think about how you can develop the worst ideas and the incredible ideas will follow!

17 WHERE DO IDEAS COME FROM?

To be able to develop new ideas and exciting projects we need to find ideas somewhere. I often get ideas when I see something that doesn't work very well. My brain starts working, and the next minute there's an idea in my head.

Ideas also come to me when I have just woken up in the morning and nothing else is clogging up the brain. They come to me when I'm travelling. Sometimes they pop up when I'm half asleep on the tube. Ideas turn up when I'm studying what's going on around me. I think *What's next?* I try to read the future, and then an idea pops up. Ideas are necessary. Look after all your ideas and some of them will blossom in the future.

Ideas often come from lack of resources. When there is not enough time, money and man-hours, you have to become creative. New ideas are often part of the answer.

When an idea is new, you need to look after it. Don't share it with negative people when it's just born or they'll kill your self-confidence and imagination. You need to let it grow stronger, and when your idea is strong enough, you can then share it with others.

In digital development you have to be creative and find new solutions to your problems. If you're unlucky, you're working in an environment where you don't have much time for reflection. This is very counterproductive and not good for you or your team's creativity at all.

HOW TO GENERATE NEW IDEAS

1. New ideas and good decisions will not come to you if you don't take time to reflect.

2. You will get new ideas from taking action. From action comes a result.

3. Some people believe the Universe or God or Source is sending them ideas.

4. Speaking to others is a great way to open up your mind.

5. Everything you do to create new thinking patterns will give you new ideas.

18 ARE YOU KILLING IDEAS BY PURPOSE OR BY MISTAKE?

I believe that many people and organisations are killing great ideas at an early stage. Again, an effective tool to get around this is the 'Yes and...', and training everyone in the idea development process as great ideas have a tendency to hide among the bad and mediocre ideas.

Anyone can come up with a normal, average idea; that's not a problem. But it's when you're expanding your thinking and dare to come up with something new and unfamiliar that you'll come up with a unique idea that will assure your future success.

If you're working on a marketing campaign, how are you going to come up with amazing ideas? Are you even trying to come up with amazing ideas? Or are you happy with staying in your organisation's comfort zone?

Is your organisation trying to build new partnerships? You're always out on the dating market and you want to work with other fun and inspiring companies. How far away from your comfort zone do you dare to go?

One way to expand your thinking is having small regular workshops in which you aim to create crazy ideas and you're also going to explore those crazy ideas. It is fun to do this, but it takes a determined team to get it working. Warning! It will feel weird at the start because you're challenging your normal thinking patterns.

An idea needs time to grow and many new concepts feel very strange when you start working on developing them. I'll say it again. The way you use your language is going to define how your ideas develop. Another big factor is how you're welcoming new thinking in your team.

SOME COMMON WAYS TO KILL AN IDEA IN ITS EARLY STAGES

- Yes, but... This 'Yes, but...' is the most common way to kill ideas. Often you hear: 'Yes, I like it, but when we tried that two years ago we got very little response.' The word 'but' is almost always followed by a negative comment. And this tiny comment can kill the energy that the idea had for a start.

- 'We don't have a budget for that this year.' I heard this many times when I was working in the corporate world. Budget thinking is limiting our belief that something is possible. Often there is money available; you just have to be a bit of a detective. And remember that all organisations are looking for great ideas, and this one might be one to help you to move forward to the next level. Budgets are there to help organisations to plan for the next year. You use them to make sure you can pay your employees and expenses for the next 12 months ahead, and they're there to consider the investments that are in the pipeline. Budgets are not there to stop people from innovating. If your finance director says no to your idea due to budget restrictions, you need to sharpen your arguments and get some more people on board to support you. Even in the most anti-innovating environments there is money lurking around that you can use; it just takes some motivation to find it.

- One way to very efficiently kill an idea is to say 'Mr Big Boss will never approve it.' Some people make themselves into messengers for their bosses and say that the idea will never be accepted. Sometimes that might be true, but if you have a great idea you can't let that stop you.

- Lack of time. We all have 168 hours per week, and time is one of the few things that all humans have exactly the same amount of. Lack of time is a great excuse if you're not interested in investigating how an idea can change your life or business. The solution is to change your priorities and make time in your busy agenda.

- If you're doing a return on investment calculation too early, you will probably put people off. Yes, it's very important to focus our time and money on ideas that will give much in return. But the truth is that many bestselling products didn't pass this test at first. The product or service might have been ahead of time, and then of course it's impossible to calculate sales figures for the future. An idea, product or service might need to mature in its own pace, and when the market is ready, BOOM! All the money and time invested comes back to you.

CREATIVE LEADERSHIP PRINCIPLES

· Bad and wonderful ideas can look exactly the same in the beginning. You need to build on them and develop them further to tell them apart. To discover the great ideas, you need to give space for the bad to exist as well.

· Let your idea grow strong and only share it with people you trust to start with. When it's stronger, you can share it with more people.

· Dare to make mistakes.

· Always learn new things and develop yourself.

19 HOW TO DEVELOP AN IDEA AND KEEP IT ALIVE

We have many more resources available around us than we normally can see. One of the best ways to discover them is to be open and use the 'Yes and...' principles. The people you have around you might have the solution you are looking for.

Be aware of your thought patterns. Are you trying to change your way of thinking and broaden the way you see your world? Awareness about yourself will help you to not say no to an idea from the start just because you are not familiar with how it can work.

When you invite your colleagues or friends to give feedback to your own idea in the early conception stages, it means that they can contribute to its success and survival. The next priority must then be to encourage them to give feedback and to use the 'Yes and...' phrase tool or principles. The best way to do that is to always use that principle when listening to their ideas. Always work on building and keeping trust among your colleagues. When the trust is gone, it takes a long time to rebuild it.

Just knowing that the next big thing that is going to move you forward will have a new shape and form compared to the past will help you to be prepared for it when it's there. Not changing is the biggest risk and you might end up being institutionalised.

An idea doesn't have to be perfect to be tested. You can develop an idea, product or service until it is 80% perfect and then test it on your customers. Early feedback can help you to make it perfect. Holding back too long because someone will have an opinion is not going to make anything perfect.

Great ideas and new combinations can come fast and be easy to develop. Some of them will need more time and imagination. Give your ideas the time they need. Some of them just need to grow up, while others are ripe and ready to use immediately.

DO YOU LOVE OLD IDEAS?

Ideas and new projects can arise from many different sources. When you're developing ideas, they don't have to be new and never explored before by someone else. Even though it feels great to come up with something new that has never been done before; copying is permitted. You can reuse an old idea and bring it alive in a new context.

Sofie says: *Ideas that already have been used by someone else are always worth exploring. It might work for your organisation as well.*

One of my personal favourites that used an old concept is the TV programme *Strictly Come Dancing.* The idea for this series came from an old TV programme about ballroom dancing. By adding the celebrity factor they made it more exciting and fun. The programme has been sold throughout the world and is one of the biggest TV success stories ever. An old idea combined with a new idea became a huge success.

There is nothing to be ashamed of if you do something that others have done before you.

I've heard many times that: 'Copy from one and it's plagiarism; copy from two and it's research'.

Look around you and see what others are doing. Can you learn from them? Your biggest competitors might be your best teachers. When you give the idea your personal input, the outcome will look and feel differently.

If an idea is a great idea in the 'normal' offline world, it may well be a great idea in the online world. We have endless opportunities to combine old ideas and concepts with digital and social media. In digital and social media there are thousands of different recipes that have been cooked by all kind of organisations, some very successful and others not so successful. If you think that your message is right and that your audience will like it then why not try them out?

20 CONFLICTS ARE GOOD FOR YOUR CREATIVITY

When you are developing an idea, a new business or a new product, you'll come to a stage when you and the people you are working with will disagree. You have different opinions and are putting your view of the world on the table. What matters in the end is how you're solving the problems and moving forward. There is a solution for most problems.

Conflicts can be good. Try to understand how the other people think and you'll open up your mind and understand the world around you better.

Sofie says: *"You are responsible for the energy*
you bring into the room, even when
you are in a conflict with someone."

- Conflicts will help you to get a discussion started and you can start dealing with the issues and reach a solution.

- The less you judge the situation the more open you are to seeing a new solution. Spend time with people who you don't always agree with; you will learn a lot in the process. The less you judge people the more opportunities you'll see about how you can work together.

- Whenever you're in a conflict, focus on the issue not the person. If you focus on the person and attack her/ him, you may burn bridges. And burnt bridges can be very difficult to repair. It takes a long time to build confidence and trust, and you can ruin it in just one moment.

- When you act in a way you believe is open and honest, the people around you will see this and respect you. If you have a hidden agenda, people will sense it and this will bite you in the bum sooner or later.

- Sometimes it feels like people are working against you. Often they do that because they are not in the right place or have their own issues. If you put on your 'leadership hat', you might be able to help this person find something else to do. This could be another role in your company or somewhere else. People who are involved in activities they enjoy aren't seeking problems and conflicts.

- When you have a conflict with a person, sit down and talk about the problem. Don't bring up what has happened in the past. If you never bring the current conflict to the forefront, it's likely that it will never heal. Talk, communicate and show your feelings. It's ideal to meet up with the other person. If this is not possible, use your phone to call them (don't text). Never email about conflicts; you can make a suggestion in the email to meet up, but don't have a long discussion in an email. People pay attention to different things in an email and you'll misunderstand each other.

One of my former Finnish colleagues used this expression: 'Put the cat on the table.' It means: get to the point and discuss the problem. The Finns have a very straightforward way of communicating. You might find this a bit scary depending on your culture, but it can be worth a try. Clean the air and get rid of the negative feelings and let new positive energy in.

If you want to get on well in your life, I think it is important to resolve conflicts with people around you. And sometimes you need to break ties with people who are not good for you. Let go of them and move on in your life with the people that give you energy and inspiration.

I love the quote I have on my Facebook profile: 'Let us be grateful to people who make us happy. They are the charming gardeners who make our souls blossom.'

CREATIVE LEADERSHIP PRINCIPLES

- Be present in both mind and body.

- Listen and tune in to what people are telling you.

- Learn more about creativity.

- Use positive language and give your colleagues a lot of positive feedback.

- Interact with your partners and customers. Let them contribute to your products and services.

- Use your online network to create new opportunities. Let your friends share your content and help you spread the word about what you're doing.

- You must prevent yourself from being a person or organisation who says no to new ideas. Be aware about what comes out of your mouth.

- If you don't watch out, you will find your organisation being an old institution that is not responsive to anything new. And that is a true nightmare.

- You're responsible for the energy you bring into the room.

21 SETTING YOUR CONDITIONS FOR CREATIVITY: SELF CARE

If you want to stay creative, a good start is to recognise what makes you tense, stressed and makes you feel disempowered. Being tense and stressed is a way to efficiently block your natural thoughts.

Think about yourself. Consider what is making you feel less creative. You will know from experience what is draining your creativity and energy. I call this part setting your conditions for creativity — essentially looking at what is going to make you blossom. Conditions for creativity are anything that maximises the chances in reaching a desired goal.

Some of my personal conditions for staying creative are: good sleep, exercise a few times per week and time to relax. Also, I know that if I've not done anything that's fun for a long time my creativity is gone with the wind. I have to look after myself before I help others, and if I forget to do that my creativity works on low speed.

Having good conditions in place for creativity to grow reminds us that we're not robots but humans with feelings and vulnerabilities. We're all unique and the conditions for creativity that we allow to exist in our life are expressing who we are and what we need to be our best. So each person requires different conditions. Maintaining our personal conditions for creativity is putting the oil in a machine. We need them to function well and we need new oil too every now and then.

Remind yourself daily to talk to yourself gently. If a machine does not work because of lack of oil, you would not scream at it 'Work now!' Instead, you would refill the oil and let it start over again.

If you have a horrible headache, are tired and have not eaten well in the last 24 hours, it's likely that your creativity is not in top form. Don't kick yourself when you're not feeling great. Your creativity will come back to you.

A person in the design industry I met at one of my workshops told me that she was always working on new projects that should go live soon. She told me that she often felt as if she could not function and that her creativity was very low. She was in this creative role and felt pressured that she should be super creative.

We spoke about her concerns and it turned out that she felt as if she didn't get enough recognition from her colleagues and friends.

I asked her who her biggest supporters and sponsors were. She identified them and then I encouraged her to ask them to give her more positive feedback and encouragement. After she had done this, she felt much better about her projects and she knew she had accountability partners who would support her and give her feedback even if she didn't feel great. The others who didn't give her positive feedback didn't matter any longer as she was already feeling great with the feedback she got.

For some people it can help them to be creative to watch less TV. Others will be more creative by relaxing and having coffee with friends more often. I can't tell you what's best for you. You need to get to know yourself better to understand this. Do be aware that your conditions for creativity might change as you grow as a person. What was right last year might not be right this year.

When I was a student, I studied with a friend who was very creative and had a strict routine that he had to follow every day to be able to function. He was inner world-focused. When we met up again recently, I could see that he had changed. He now focuses more on the outer world and the people he has around him. His conditions for being a creative human being have changed. It is not the routine that makes him creative any longer but the people he meets and works with. His situation has changed — from living in a student environment to working for a big newspaper. This made his life very different and his conditions changed with him.

EXERCISE: SETTING YOUR CONDITIONS FOR CREATIVITY

Compare situations when you have been very creative and other circumstances when you felt drained and tired. What was it that was different?

An example can be: very creative and inspired — 'I felt rested and had a good breakfast.' Not creative — 'I was feeling stressed and insecure; I had been sleeping badly for several days in a row.'

Now think about your conditions for creativity: what is it that blocks you and what makes you blossom? Make a drawing where you describe what is important for you to stay creative. This is your personal reminder of what's important to you. Don't use words. Drawings are much more efficient and will stay in your memory better. You're also using more parts of the brain when drawing.

If you feel that going to a comedy show is great for you, draw a big laughing mouth. If it's jogging, draw a jogger. If you need more sleep, draw a bed.

Keep this piece of art close to you for a while and remind yourself that you have to do these things that are good for your inner creativity. Put it on your fridge and make sure you follow them.

You have to have fun, talk to your friends, do things you're entertained by that's going to nurture your creativity, whatever that is — musicals, theatre, trips. Remember to do things that YOU think are fun and inspiring. It all starts within you!

PART FOUR

THE LEADERSHIP CHALLENGE

"Listen to anyone with an original idea, no matter how absurd it may sound at first. If you put fences around people, you get sheep. Give people the room they need."

William McKnight, 3M President

22 FOLLOW AND LEAD
- LEAD AND FOLLOW

In my career I've worked with some great people who have taught me many useful things. I've developed my knowledge, skills and confidence and also changed my attitude to problems when working with them. They inspired me to follow them in the journey they were on, and I also felt that I could inspire them in return to make the outcome better.

Over 2000 years ago Aristotle said, 'He who cannot be a good follower cannot be a good leader.' I've done my own interpretation of the quote.

We all have something new to learn every day, top leaders as well as young students. Great leaders are humble and open to learn new insights. That keeps them going and it keeps them ahead of everyone else. This is why you have to follow others. Let other people who know their stuff teach you new skills and give you new insights.

Another aspect is what I heard several years ago by a military person. 'The troop has to know what to do even if its leader is dead.' This means that you have to know what to do in the next step and what was in the plan even if no one will give you an order. The leader has to make sure that you have the right training to be able to continue working towards the goal without microinstructions.

I believe you have to follow great leaders to be able to learn how to lead. Study what they do and how it works. Your leadership abilities expand every time you have the chance to work with other leaders. Learn from what they have done, what worked and then, when you have the chance to lead, you will have a better idea of what will work for you in different situations.

If you look around and see some great people, engage them in the creative process. Learn from them. You still have a lot to learn whatever age you are. To be surrounded by talented people is a gift; they will make sure you develop yourself.

Sofie says: *"Follow and learn from others and you'll expand your own abilities to become a better leader."*

To be a leader of a digital team can be a challenge, but the more you're aware of the creativity principles the better you and your team will perform. Digital media is developing fast and you have to develop your knowledge to be constantly up to date. If you're good at the basics and know how the online world works, you will find it reasonably easy to keep up with the new information flow.

HEADS UP OR HEADS DOWN. HOW ARE YOU AS A LEADER IN A CRITICAL MOMENT?

Often it is tempting to just keep your mouth shut and keep on 'doing your job' when there is a conflict or disagreement. When there is change and turbulence around us, it feels safe to pretend that nothing is going on. Do you recognise this scenario? Have you done it?

Sofie says: *"Creative leaders stick their necks out in critical situations. They challenge decisions and want to understand how they will influence the future."*

Many individuals who are climbing the career ladder are waiting to say what they think until they reach the top. You know, that moment when you're allowed to do it. I don't think it works this way; people on the top who challenge what is going on around them have done this on many occasions in their career. They started to do this early. And you need to do this so that you can be strong on the top. The higher you climb the more conflicts, change and turbulence you need to be able to handle. So speak up early on and grow into your leadership role.

"Nobody ever became a leader because
they focused on the problem."
Sofie Sandell

Another thing that is important to identify is that there are not that many people reaching the top. So we need all people in an organisation to have a voice and influence decision making. Keeping quiet will not help the organisation move forward, or yourself.

To gain respect you have to demonstrate that the people around you can count on you in tough times. That you will stand up for yourself and what you believe in. A marketing team I trained had a problem with a manager that used to reprimand her team in public.

It was a problem that got bigger and bigger; if anyone reprimands you in public on a regular basis, you can get very upset and lose your energy. What the manager did when punishing her team in public was tell everyone that she was not a person to trust, and without trust it's very hard to be a good leader.

Sofie says: *"Leadership is about looking for better solutions for the people around you. Continual improvement can only happen when leaders show the way and dare to take on conflict."*

DO YOU DARE TO ...

- take the risk of being wrong?
- be unpopular? (maybe just for a short period)
- make a difference for the future?
- follow your gut feeling?

We all need to improve our communications skills with others and also to listen to ourselves. To change the world around us we need to be strong in our gut feelings. Our intuition will tell us what is right. And we have to work with our own values that are giving us direction in our life every day.

We need to have the courage to take on conflict. Being able to weather the storm and not take things personally are the hallmarks of a great leader.

23 WHO IS AN EXPERT?

I often call people I meet who seem to know a lot about a specific area — an 'expert'. In the digital world there are loads of experts, as in the medical profession. Some doctors are brain surgeons; others focus on the gut and some on the skin. It's the same in the digital world; people have different expertise. The experts may confuse you, but they might also open your world to new possibilities.

Many people I've met say, 'No, don't call me an expert.' Well, if you're knowledgeable in an area or subject, I may well call you an expert.

I then ask, 'Why can't I call you an expert?' And I start thinking, You're pretty good at what you're doing, so is it dangerous to be called an expert? Will anyone punish you if you call yourself an expert or are you not allowing yourself to be the expert? Shall I call you an Authority, Specialist, Wizard or simply Knowledgeable Person?

An expert for me is a person who can make a critical decision quickly about a problem.

1. They can give good advice in the moment you need it.

2. They have made many mistakes and have learnt ways to fix them in a very narrow area.

3. They can recommend where you should go to search for more information.

4. They have historical knowledge about the subject.

5. They can see where the future is heading and they know what's around the corner.

What all experts have in common is their passion for the topic, whatever that might be. Another aspect is that they know so much about their topic that many answers you'll get from them are neither black nor white. They will give you their point of view and also tell you about other possibilities.

When someone calls you an expert, smile, receive the compliment and say thank you.

24 HOW TO MANAGE CREATIVE PEOPLE

Creativity is a mystery, as is love. If you're managing creative people and you want the best out of them, you need to let go of many preconceptions about how people 'are'. New innovations and creative ideas will come alive if you are creating an environment that is helping people to show off their creativity. You have to create space for the creativity mystery to exist and let go of many of your own insecurities that you might feel inside you. These insecurities might stop yourself and the people you work with to perform your best as a team.

I would recommend you read the book *Creativity: Flow and the Psychology of Discovery and Invention* by Mihaly Csikszentmihalyi [HarperCollins 1996]. He makes some good points in it about creativity, creative people and flow. It is his research about flow that made him know to me many years ago.

According to Csikszentmihalyi [1996]:

- Creative people have a lot of physical energy and they do take time to rewind and relax. Their energy level can be totally different from day to day.

- Creative individuals tend to be smart but at the same time naïve.

- Creative people are both playful and disciplined at the same time.

- Creative people are full of imagination and they have a gut feeling for what's around the corner. Being able to use your fantasy and imagination whilst being rooted in reality is a trait of creative individuals.

- When a person who is fully using their creative abilities is developing an idea, they tend to be introverted for a period of time. Then when the new creative idea is developed, they want to go out and meet other people and share the idea with them. Creative people are both introverted and extroverted.

His research shows that it's important for us to not judge people too quickly; you never know if you are working with a creative genius. All people have some sort of talent and if you want them to share these with you, you need to treat people well and accept them as they are.

I believe one of the most dangerous things you can do in any human relationship is to place someone in a box: you are like that; you always do this; typical you... When you are putting people in a box, it's not good for their creativity or flow, and neither is it good for yours.

Love, people and relationships are all big mysteries. Treat them nicely and you'll get much more in return.

HOW TO MANAGE AND KEEP GEEKS HAPPY

Some of the most creative companies in the world were created by geeks. Remember Apple, Pixar and the like. IT and digital teams are very dependent on experts — geeks, programmers and developers who'll create magic solutions for your website and digital tools. To keep them happy, it's even more important for you to know about the creative process and how to handle ideas. I've worked with a lot of different people and some of them have been a bit geekier than others and often they were very proud to be geeks.

I don't think it's a big difference between managing geeks and other staff members, but you should be aware that those geeks who don't think your web environment is interesting enough are likely to move on pretty swiftly.

You always want your team members to perform their best, to come up with great solutions to all your problems. If the geeks don't like you, they will not come up with the best solution. And you'll not provide your customers with the best solution. If the geeks find you annoying as a leader, they are more likely than any other employees to leave your organisation.

Very geeky people can be introvert, and you might not have super social conversations with them. The reality is that some people are more introvert and some people talk too much. That's life. You as a leader have to adopt your style and be nice to everyone in your team. That will help you, and people will step forward to work with you.

> *"You can't tell a software developer what to do.*
> *You're paying them for inventing new things.*
> *Not managing the details in their work."*
> **Zoe Cunningham**

Training is always a valuable tool if you wish to keep your geeky team members happy. Most people love to learn new stuff, especially knowledge hungry geeks. Give them free programming books on Amazon. Let them use and improve their skills as much as possible. I'm a bit geeky myself and I was once hired to work in the web department but ended up doing mostly administration. I moved on and got a new job.

Smart people want to work with other smart people and be in a team that gets on socially. Make sure that good communication processes are set up and that the entire team knows how and where communication can be shared. Remote working will also help keep your team members happy.

One great way to give compliments to your team is to make your team members shine in front of others. They will love you for that, even if they don't say it out loud. The simple truth is that we all want to work with people who make us feel great and valuable — geeky or not. But in the world of digital you have to work well with geeks because they have mind power over the magic solutions that will help you make money in the future.

To keep a creative environment alive you need to avoid the HIPO syndrome as much as possible. This stands for Highest Income Person's Opinion or the person with most power. If you make technical decisions based on advice from a non-techie then the developers won't do a good job.

A huge global company chose to go with an old enterprise resource planning (ERP) solution five years ago. They made big investments and started the implementation. One year into the project it turned out that Oracle stopped upgrading and supporting the solution they had bought. They lost several technical people and a lot of enthusiasm in the project. Nobody wanted to work with a technical system that had very little support and development in the future.

Why do you think they were finding themselves in this situation? The management didn't listen to the advice they got from the technical developers. If they had done that, they would have invested in another

ERP product. To listen to feedback and an ability to learn are musts for creative leaders.

LEARN FROM THE LEADERS AROUND YOU

I've been to many networking events and I've even written a business thesis on the subject of networking and professional development. Look at your network, all the people you know. Who has had most impact in your life? Who has helped you to move forward? Who has opened new doors for you?

Is it the world's famous heroes who have been influencing you? Is it the amazing people winning awards and prizes for their talents, such as the Oscar and Noble Peace Prize winners?

No, it is not the famous heroes who make the biggest mark in our lives. It's our family, teachers and friends who are shaping us. Your identity is shaped by the people you meet and what happens to you. We're our stories, and they are shaping us and how we see the world around us, how we think, how we move forward and how we deal with our challenges.

I've had a handful of people who have influenced me a lot. And I'll always be grateful for having them in my life; you're the best teachers I possibly could have had. Be grateful for the people you have met. Be grateful for what you've learnt. Be grateful for all great teachers you've had so far. And keep your door open to let new people into your life.

And by the way, who remembers any of the Noble Prize winners from last year? (I don't remember a single one...)

BUILDING YOUR NETWORK ONLINE AND THE IMPORTANCE OF TRUST

There's a big lack of trust in the world today. Many consumers think that they can't trust any big brands. We're not sure who we can trust in our jobs. Relationships are complex and we don't know who's on our side.

It's very easy to lose trust in the digital world; it only takes one email or an inappropriate Facebook comment. I once had a business contact forward an email to one of our partners in the project we were working in. In the email we were discussing the project and its problems. This email was forwarded to a person in our partner team. I found it very hard to trust the person who forwarded this email again.

Another way to break trust is to make offensive comments online on someone's social profile. The number one rule is: don't do things online that will be offensive in the office or in the pub. The same social rules apply both online and offline.

When meeting new people online, we're more likely to find people we're clicking with. Look at the success with online dating. I've many friends and acquaintances who met their love online. Being social is a fundamental human need, so is dating and getting a partner.

Use LinkedIn and update your profile. Write something that makes people interested in you and what you do. When someone is looking for an expert or a person with a certain skill, they are going to search on Google, YouTube and LinkedIn. Your profile might be the one they see and then you get to know a new person.

I've got new connections from all over the world from using Facebook, LinkedIn and Twitter. Some of them have led to business and new friendships. If you want to build a stronger network, use social media and the digital solutions available.

AFTERWORD

I sincerely hope that you have appreciated this book and learnt more about creativity in business and the digital world. With the digital tools discussed and your creativity you can influence more people, improve your work flow and get more things done.

When we're scared of trying something new, we don't dare to change the way we are working, and this is perhaps because that is how we've always done it. We say no to great ideas and it's hard to see new opportunities because of the thick fog in front of us.

Make new technology your best friend and learn how you can use the platforms that are available, and you and your business will be more successful. One of the beautiful aspects of digital is that it's very easy to build new relationships. You don't have to know each other in person to start a project. You can build on each other's connections and platforms and create wealth from there.

Digital tools are helping you to leave a legacy, to make an impact. Your words and your content will matter to others. You don't have to wait for permission to write something online; you can start sharing your thoughts today.

Handle the ideas and the creative force you have around you with care and you'll become a strong leader who inspires others. A person who gives inspiration to others is indeed a leader. Sometimes leadership has to do with a title, but often it's the action taken by a person which makes him or her a leader.

I use creativity in my life every day. I am reminding myself about my conditions for creativity and that they are there every day. I practice relearning daily, revalidate and re-inspire myself, and thus boost my creativity. Work on your conditions for creativity; get to know what makes you happy.

Never say that you know everything and that you don't need help. I think this is one of the most dangerous things you can do. We're learning something new in all relationships and partnerships we are in. Be coachable, a person who's always learning new insights, and you'll become a digital leader. When you're in this frame of mind, you're going to perform your best.

I would love to connect with you online and hear about your work and progress. Please send me a request via LinkedIn; search for 'Sofie Sandell' and you'll find me. In the future I hope to meet you at one of my workshops. And you'll find me on Twitter and many other social media networks as well.

Be bold and show the world that you are a creative digital leader!

Sofie Sandell

BRING THE DIGITAL AND CREATIVE LEADERSHIP PRINCIPLES INTO YOUR ORGANISATION

- The Digital Leadership Masterclass
- Social Media Workshop for Leaders and Influencers
- Creativity Workshop: Creative Thinking for Businesses
- Creativity Workshop: Creativity in Business and Leadership Development
- 1-2-1 Digital and Social Media Training and Coaching

Positive and profound changes take place when you, your employees, colleagues, managers and students are experiencing the principles live in a workshop.

You will learn together how to shape your language and behaviour so it will help you to work better as a team, and become more efficient. When you learn how to listen to each other and treat new ideas better, you are going to achieve a much better result.

Workshops are ideal for groups such as:

- Small businesses
- Corporate teams
- Managers and executives
- Sales and marketing teams
- Corporate conferences
- Students and educators
- Trade associations and its membership
- Health care providers
- Government
- Local authorities

All people will benefit from learning more about idea development, creativity and the digital opportunities. Develop yourself, improve your relationships, and move your team and business to a new level.

Read more at www.sofiesandell.com and contact Sofie Sandell at hello@sofiesandell.com

APPENDIX

65 QUESTIONS TO BOOST YOUR CREATIVITY

I am a very creative person and I've been working in some organisations where I've been very happy because I've been able to express that creativity. One of the key aspects in the great organisations I've been working in is good relationships and that nobody wanted to stop my creativity; they let me play, test and fail. Whenever I've been working in a 'control-freak' environment, it has driven me crazy and I felt slightly depressed.

It is the synergies between several people that are leading to the next 'Big Thing', not a single person's effort. What counts in the long run is the effort that many people have been giving to the project over a long time. After a while you'll harvest the fruits that came out of the project and you will all feel that you've accomplished something together.

One thing that is driving the creative process forward is the way you ask questions. Ask the right questions and the answers will come to you. I often suggest to teams that they have to ask themselves the right questions to create better content and output. Questions will drive the creative process forward.

And questions also create new ideas and content in your life.

"You only get what you ask for,
nothing more nothing less."
Sofie Sandell

If you ask the right questions, you have the power. When you ask good questions, you are going to cross-pollinate your and other people's ideas much easier.

If you would like to change your results, you have to change the questions you are asking yourself and your team. The answers you get will take you on a journey.

"Words are, of course, the most powerful
drug used by mankind."
Rudyard Kipling

I've collected a number of questions to ask yourself, your team, your organisation and the ecosystem.

When you are asking yourself these questions, you are opening up your mind. And an open mind means a mind that is more action-oriented and a mind that sees new solutions.

Read them every now and then to remind yourself about what you would like to achieve in your team and to see if there is anything you can do differently.

QUESTIONS TO ASK YOURSELF

Assess what you are doing and see what you can do to be more creative and to be better at inspiring other people. Here are some questions to ask yourself.

1. Have I done something I love and enjoy in the last week?

2. What is my current attitude to my creativity?

3. Do I encourage the people I meet to be creative?

4. How many conscious thoughts have I had today?

5. How can I take a different route when looking at a problem?

6. Have I given anyone a compliment today?

7. Do I need to spend more time by myself?

8. Am I doing this because I want recognition from others or because I want to?

9. Am I doing this for the greater good or for myself?

10. How would my team like me to communicate with them?

11. Can I do anything differently in my communication?

12. Is the tone in my emails nice and friendly?

13. Am I open to listening to ideas that my colleagues want to discuss?

14. How much do I know about the idea development process? Do I need to improve my skills?

15. Am I judging this because of my previous experiences or am I open to learning something new?

16. Do I have too much experience of bad projects in this area, so I am closing my mind?

17. How much do I know about the topic? Do I need to gain more knowledge before I make a decision?

18. Do I routinely like my own ideas better than my colleague's ideas?

19. Who are the people I know that are normally nice to new ideas? Can I beta test my idea on them first?

20. Is what I am doing in my work going to make a difference in anyone's life? If so, how?

21. Do I steal other people's ideas and present them as my own?

22. Am I focusing on the people who are inspired by my idea or the people who are thrilled at my failure?

23. Am I punishing people who have made mistakes in private or in public? If you do this in public, you are showing that you are not a person to trust.

24. What have I learnt when I have failed in the past?

25. How do I speak about my failures? (How you speak about your failure will determine how much risk your colleagues are going to take in the next project.)

26. Am I often telling my team that they have to work faster?

27. If I had no budget restriction would I do this?

28. If I had no budget at all, how would I run this project?

29. Have I set my conditions for creativity?

30. What is draining my energy?

31. What is giving me energy?

QUESTIONS TO YOUR TEAM

We all learn by making mistakes. Do you remember when you were a baby and learnt to walk? Your parents didn't scream at you when you fell, but encouraged you to take a new step. We are learning new things from the day we are born until the day we die. The more people we have around us, screaming at us not to take that step, the less likely we are to take risks — big or small.

What will always stay in the minds of people are the kind words of encouragement that they heard, and it might be the echo of these words that will make people jump higher. So use your language in a way that will make people work more efficiently, and avoid harsh language.

32. How are you? (Ask your colleagues how they are doing and you have created a connection. A simple, easy and clean question to ask.)

33. Do the people in your team know each other or not?

34. How can you do something to get to know each other better?

35. Does your team like to show off what they have done?

36. Is your team a popular team in your organisation?

37. Will other people take notice when you have done something great?

38. Are you happy to brag about your team's performance?

39. Do you know how the idea development process works?

40. Are the team members keeping their promises?

41. How do people in your team give each other feedback?

42. Does everyone know 'Why' what you do is important?

43. How is the health of your team in general? Many sick days?

44. Do you trust each other? Are you gossiping too much? (If the trust is gone, you don't have much to build on.)

45. Is your team feeling that they are always working under pressure? Are you contributing to the stress in any way?

46. How important are your deadlines? Do you remember why they are there or are they there because of habit?

47. If your deadline is there because of habit, you'll have problems communicating why. And 'why' is the most important question to ask when you are in a hurry.

48. How do you remind your team that you are striving for a creative working environment? Routines, symbols, emails or in your spoken words?

QUESTIONS TO ASK YOUR ORGANISATION

49. What kind of products do we need to survive in the future?

50. What kind of people and skills do we need to attract in the future?

51. What are we doing really well?

52. Where do we put too much attention?

53. Are we having too many meetings?

54. How do we describe the company culture?

55. Is it easy to get support for new ideas?

56. Can we create more partnerships within the organisation and with other organisations?

57. How can we make things simpler and clearer?

58. Do we have too many processes?

59. Do we have too few processes?

QUESTIONS TO ASK THE WHOLE ECOSYSTEM

60. Do you know which other organisations are part of your bigger ecosystem?

61. Do you know who your key suppliers are that you can't be without?

62. Who are you a key supplier to?

63. Do you know each other well?

64. Do you work well together?

65. Are you working together in your system to improve the ecosystem or are you working solo?

ABOUT THE AUTHOR

 Sofie Sandell is an entrepreneur with interests spanning from technology and leadership to art and sailing. Sofie's passion is to teach and inspire people on how to become digital and creative leaders. Sofie is an author, speaker, trainer and university lecturer. In 2013 she spoke about 'Digital Leadership - empowering new ideas' at TEDxUCL. She is also a regular contributor to the technology radio show #TechTalkfest where she talks about all things digital. Sofie has had a number of leadership roles in non-governmental organisations and in 2011 she was awarded the Freedom of the City of London in recognition of her service to the city.

Working in big and small organisations in the last 15 years, Sofie has been exploring not only what makes organisations and teams work well together, but also what makes them perform above and beyond expectation. Sofie has also been involved in Junior Chamber International (JCI) on a local and national level, a global network of young professionals whose mission is to empower young people to create positive change and offers members hands-on leadership experience.

By pushing boundaries in her research on creativity she has been exploring its many aspects, from creativity in business, improvisational theatre to creative art and Buddhist creative awareness.

Through these experiences Sofie has learnt the importance of trust and letting go. She has found that the most successful teams are teams that trust the creative process, support each other through the process and don't play the blame-game if things don't go as expected. As Sofie says in this book, all ideas start out the same but you can never tell where an idea will end up; you have to trust the process.

Sofie loves technology and she loves communicating. She believes that digital leadership is about creating better and stronger connections online and offline by using the digital tools. Sofie's favourite online networks are Facebook, LinkedIn, Twitter, MeetUp and the Harvard Business Review blog.

Sofie's clients include small and big businesses, politicians, entrepreneurs, creative professionals, company executives and CEOs who want to succeed in the digital world using their own and their team's creativity.

Sofie was born and raised in Sweden and now lives in London; she works all around the world.

To find out more about Sofie's workshops and training you can contact her at hello@sofiesandell.com.

Connect with Sofie Sandell online:

www.sofiesandell.com
Twitter.com/Soffi_Propp
www.linkedin.com/in/sofiesandell